Ethnographic Fieldwork

Full details of all our publications can be found on http://www.multilingual-matters.com, or by writing to Multilingual Matters, St Nicholas House, 31–34 High Street, Bristol BS1 2AW, UK.

Ethnographic Fieldwork
A Beginner's Guide

Jan Blommaert and Dong Jie

MULTILINGUAL MATTERS
Bristol • Buffalo • Toronto

Library of Congress Cataloging in Publication Data
A catalog record for this book is available from the Library of Congress.
Blommaert, Jan.
Ethnographic Fieldwork: A Beginner's Guide/Jan Blommaert and Dong Jie.
Includes bibliographical references and index.
1. Ethnology--Fieldwork. I. Jie, Dong, 1975- II. Title.
GN346.B56 2010
305.800723–dc22 2010021280

British Library Cataloguing in Publication Data
A catalogue entry for this book is available from the British Library.

ISBN-13: 978-1-84769-295-5 (hbk)
ISBN-13: 978-1-84769-294-8 (pbk)

Multilingual Matters
UK: St Nicholas House, 31–34 High Street, Bristol, BS1 2AW, UK.
USA: UTP, 2250 Military Road, Tonawanda, NY 14150, USA.
Canada: UTP, 5201 Dufferin Street, North York, Ontario, M3H 5T8, Canada.

The policy of Multilingual Matters/Channel View Publications is to use papers that are natural, renewable and recyclable products, made from wood grown in sustainable forests. In the manufacturing process of our books, and to further support our policy, preference is given to printers that have FSC and PEFC Chain of Custody certification. The FSC and/or PEFC logos will appear on those books where full certification has been granted to the printer concerned.

Typeset by Techset Composition Ltd., Salisbury, UK.
Printed and bound in Great Britain by Short Run Press Ltd.

Contents

Chapter 1
Introduction

It is a scary thing, isn't it: the idea of being alone 'in the field', trying to accomplish a task initially formulated as a perfectly coherent research plan with questions, methods, readings and so on – and finding out that the 'field' is a chaotic, hugely complex place. Fieldwork is the moment when the researcher climbs down to everyday reality and finds out that the rules of academia are not necessarily the same as those of everyday life. Unfortunately, the only available solution to that is unilateral adaptation by the researcher. Everyday life will never adjust to your research plan; the only way forward is to adapt your plan and ways of going about things to the rules of everyday reality. There is no magic formula for this, and this book should not – not! – be read as such.

But there are things one can do better or worse, and whichever way we look at it, fieldwork is a theorised mode of action, something in which researchers still follow certain procedures and have to follow them; something in which a particular set of actions need to be performed; and something that needs to result in a body of knowledge that can be re-submitted to rigorous, disciplined academic tactics. This book is aimed at providing some general suggestions for how to go about it, at demarcating a space in which what we do can be called 'research'. It is a complex space, not something one immediately recognises, and given the increased emphasis on fieldwork – *ethnographic* fieldwork – some things may require structured attention.

We will start with a number of observations on ethnography. These are crucial: whenever we say ethnography (and formulate fieldwork as part of that procedure) we invoke a particular scientific tradition. It is amazing to see how often that tradition is misunderstood or misrepresented. Yet, a fair understanding of it is indispensable if we want to know what our fieldwork will yield: it will yield *ethnographic data*, and such data are fundamentally different from data collected through most other approaches. Informed readers will detect in our discussion many traces of

1

the foundational work by Johannes Fabian and Dell Hymes – the two main methodologists of contemporary ethnography, whose works remain indispensable reading for anyone seriously interested in ethnography. Next, we will go through the 'sequence' usually performed in fieldwork: pre-field preparation, entering the field, observation, interviewing, data formulation, analysis, the return from the field.

One should note that we do not provide a 'do and don't' kind of guide to fieldwork. We will rather focus on more fundamental procedures of knowledge-construction. There are several purely practical guidelines for aspects of fieldwork. Fieldwork here is treated as an intellectual enterprise, a procedure that requires serious reflection *as much as* practical preparation and skill. Still, it is our hope (and silent conviction) that these reflections are, at the end of the day, very practical. One can never be good at anything when one doesn't really know what one is doing.

A second disclaimer is this. We are both linguistic anthropologists and sociolinguists; our views on ethnography and fieldwork necessarily have their roots in experiences with working on languages and linguistic/sociolinguistic phenomena. Most of the concrete examples or illustrations we provide will, consequently, relate to such issues, and we hope that the non-language-focused student will not be scared by them. An effort may be required to convert these illustrations and arguments into other topics; do try to make the effort. Throughout the book, we will also provide vignettes from Dong Jie's fieldwork on identity construction among rural migrants in Beijing. Her research, carried out between 2006 and 2009, will run through the book as a steady beat. This does not mean that Dong Jie was the only of the two authors who learned and experienced fieldwork; the trials and errors of fieldwork were also very much part of Jan's experience as a researcher. Elements from Jan's experience will occur throughout the book, especially in the final chapter. But Dong Jie's fresh materials may speak in a more authentic voice to our preferred readers: young researchers who are embarking on their first fieldwork jobs.

Finally, we want to use a motto for this text, something that provides a baseline for what follows. It's a quote from Hymes (1981: 84), occurring in an argument about the need for analytic attention to *'behavioral repertoire'* – the actual range of forms of behaviour that people display, and that makes them identifiable as members of a culture. This repertoire of individuals does not coincide with that of *the* culture in its whole: it is always a mistake to equate the resources of a language, culture or society with those of its members. Nobody possesses the full range of skills and resources, everyone has control over just parts of them, nobody is a perfect speaker of a language or a perfect member of a culture or society. In addition, Hymes alerts us to

> the small portion of cultural behavior that people can be expected to report or describe, when asked, and the much smaller portion that an average person can be expected to manifest by doing on demand.

And he caustically adds, between brackets, '*Some social research seems incredibly to assume that what there is to find out can be found out by asking*'.

Let us keep this motto in mind. People are not cultural or linguistic catalogues, and most of what we see as their cultural and social behaviour is performed without reflecting on it and without an active awareness that this is actually something they *do*. Consequently, it is not a thing they have an opinion about, nor an issue that can be comfortably put in words when you ask about it.[1] Ethnographic fieldwork is aimed at finding out things that are often not seen as important but belong to the implicit structures of people's life. Asking is indeed very often the worst possible way of trying to find out.

Note

1. Don't overlook the importance of this point. As Bourdieu reminds us in various places in his work, people *have no opinion* about most of the things that happen around them. And this is normal: there are very, very few issues in the world that are *everybody's* concern. Some forms of opinion research, and our media these days, have created an opposite image: that everyone has an opinion about everything, that we all *should* have opinions about everything, and that we all have *good* and *valid* opinions about everything.

Read up on it

Agar, M. (1995) Ethnography. In J. Verschueren, J-O. Östman and J. Blommaert (eds) *Handbook of Pragmatics: Manual* (pp. 583–590). Amsterdam: John Benjamins.

Fabian, J. (1991) Rule and process. In *Time and the Work of Anthropology* (pp. 87–109). Chur: Harwood.

Fabian, J. (1995) Ethnographic misunderstanding and the perils of context. *American Anthropologist* 97 (1), 41–50.

Fabian, J. (2001) Ethnographic objectivity: From rigor to vigor. In *Anthropology with an Attitude* (pp. 11–32). Stanford: Stanford University Press.

Chapter 2
Ethnography

Ethnography is a strange scientific phenomenon.[1] On the one hand, it can be seen as probably the only truly influential 'invention' of anthropological linguistics, having triggered important developments in social-scientific fields as diverse as pragmatics and discourse analysis, sociology and historiography and having caused a degree of attention to small detail in human interaction previously unaddressed in many fields of the social sciences.[2] At the same time, ethnography has for decades come under fire from within. Critical anthropology emerged from within ethnography, and strident critiques by, for example, Johannes Fabian (1983) and James Clifford (1988) exposed immense epistemological and ethical problems in ethnography. Their call for a historisation of *ethnographies* (rather than a singular *ethnography*) was answered by a flood of studies contextualising the work of prominent ethnographers, often in ways that critically called into question the epistemological, positive-scientific appeal so prominently voiced in the works of, for example, Griaule, Boas or Malinowski (see e.g. Darnell, 1998; Stocking, 1992). So, whereas ethnography is by all standards a hugely successful enterprise, its respectability has never matched its influence in the social sciences.

'True' ethnography is rare – a fact perhaps deriving from its controversial status and the falsification of claims to positive scientificity by its founding fathers. More often than not, ethnography is perceived as a *method* for collecting particular types of data and thus as something that can be added, like the use of a computer, to different scientific procedures and programs. Even in anthropology, ethnography is often seen as a synonym for description. In the field of language, ethnography is popularly perceived as a technique and a series of propositions by means of which something can be said about 'context'. Talk can thus be separated from its context, and whereas the study of talk is a matter for linguistics, conversation analysis or discourse analysis, the study of context is a matter for ethnography (see Blommaert, 2001 for a fuller discussion and references; Gumperz & Hymes, 1972 is the classic text on this). What we notice in such discussions and treatments of ethnography is a reduction of ethnography to *fieldwork*, but naïvely, in the sense that the critical epistemological issues buried in seemingly simple fieldwork practices are not taken into account. Fieldwork/ethnography is perceived as *description*: an account of facts and experiences captured under the label of 'context', but in itself often un- or under-contextualised.

It is against this narrow view that we want to pit our argument, which will revolve around the fact that ethnography *can as well* be seen as a 'full' intellectual programme far richer than just a matter of description. Ethnography, we will argue, involves a *perspective* on language and communication, including ontology and an epistemology, both of which are of significance for the study of language in society, or better, of language *as well as* of society. Interestingly, this programmatic view of ethnography emerges from critical voices from within ethnography. Rather than destroying the ethnographic project, critiques such as the ones developed by Fabian (1979, 1983, 1995) and Hymes (1972, 1996) have added substance and punch to the programme.

Ethnography as a Paradigm

A first correction that needs to be made to the widespread image of ethnography is that right from the start, it was far more than a complex of fieldwork techniques. Ever since its beginnings in the works of Malinowski and Boas, it was part of a total programme of scientific description and interpretation, comprising not only technical, methodical aspects (Malinowskian fieldwork) but also, for example, cultural relativism and behaviourist–functionalist theoretical underpinnings. Ethnography was the scientific apparatus that put communities, rather than human kind, on the map, focusing attention on the complexity of separate social units, the intricate relations between small features of a single system usually seen as in balance.[3] In Sapirian linguistics, folklore and descriptive linguistics went hand in hand with linguistic classification and historical-genetic treatments of cultures and societies. Ethnography was an approach in which systems were conceived as non-homogeneous, composed of a variety of features, and in which part–whole relationships were central to the work of interpretation and analysis. Regna Darnell's book on Boas (Darnell, 1998) contains a revealing discussion of the differences between Boas and Sapir regarding the classification of North American languages, and one of the striking things is to see how linguistic classification becomes a domain for the articulation of theories of culture and cultural dynamics, certainly in Boas' case (Darnell, 1998: 211ff). It is significant also that as ethnography became more sophisticated and linguistic phenomena were studied in greater detail and nuance, better and more mature theories of social units such as the speech community emerged (Gumperz, 1968).

So there always was more than just description in ethnography – problems of interpretation and indeed of ontology and epistemology have always figured in debates on and in ethnography, as did matters of method versus interpretation and issues of aligning ethnography with one discipline or another (linguistics versus anthropology being, for example, the issue in the Boas–Sapir debate on classification). In fact, it is our conviction that ethnography, certainly in the works of its most prominent practitioners, has always had aspirations to *theory* status. No doubt, Dell Hymes' oeuvre stands out in its attempt at retrieving the historical roots of this larger ethnographic program (Hymes, 1964, 1983) as well as at providing a firm theoretical grounding for ethnography himself (Hymes, 1972, 1996). Hymes took stock of new reflections on 'theory' produced in Chomskyan linguistics, and foregrounded the issue in ethnography as well, and in clearer and more outspoken terms than before. To Hymes, ethnography was a 'descriptive theory': an approach that was theoretical because it provided description in specific, methodologically and epistemologically grounded ways.

We will discuss some of the main lines of argument in Hymes' work at some length here, adding, at points, important elements for our understanding of ethnography as taken from Johannes Fabian's work. Fabian, like Hymes, is probably best known for his documentary work (e.g. Fabian, 1986, 1996), while his theoretical reflections have not received the attention they deserve.

To start with, a crucial element in any discussion of ethnography should be its history, for inscribed in its techniques and patterns of operation are numerous traces of its intellectual origins and background. Ethnography has its origin in anthropology, not in linguistics, nor in sociology or psychology. That means that *the basic architecture of ethnography is one that already contains ontologies, methodologies and epistemologies* that need to be situated within the larger tradition of anthropology and that do not necessarily fit the frameworks of other traditions. Central to this is *humanism*: 'It is anthropology's task to coordinate knowledge about language from the viewpoint of *man*' (Hymes, 1964: xiii). This means that language is approached as something that has a certain relevance to man, and man in anthropology is seen as a creature whose existence is narrowly linked, conditioned or determined by society, community, the group, culture.

Language from an anthropological perspective is almost necessarily captured in a functionalist epistemology, and questions about language take the shape of questions of how language works and operates for, with and by humans-as-social-beings.[4]

Let us immediately sketch some of the implications of this humanist and functionalist anthropological background to ethnography. One important consequence has to do with the *ontology*, the definition of language itself. Language is typically seen as a socially loaded and assessed tool for humans, the finality of which is to enable humans to perform as social beings. Language, in this tradition, is defined as a *resource* to be used, deployed and exploited by human beings in social life and hence socially consequential for humans. Further implications of this will be addressed below. A second important implication is about context. There is no way in which language can be 'context-less' in this anthropological tradition in ethnography. To language, there is always a particular function, a concrete shape, a specific mode of operation, and an identifiable set of relations between singular acts of language and wider patterns of resources and their functions. Language is context, it is the architecture of social behaviour itself, and thus part of social structure and social relations. To this as well we will return below.

Let us summarise what has been said so far. Central to any understanding of ethnography are its roots in anthropology. These anthropological roots provide a specific direction to ethnography, one that situates language deeply and inextricably in social life and offers a particular and distinct ontology and epistemology to ethnography. Ethnography contains a *perspective* on language which differs from that of many other branches of the study of language. It is important to remember this, and despite possible relocations and redeployments of ethnography in different theoretical frameworks, the fact that it is designed to fit an anthropological set of questions is important for our understanding of what ethnography can and cannot perform. As Hymes says, 'failure to remember can confuse or impair anthropological thinking and research, setting up false antitheses and leaving significant phenomena unstudied' (1964: xxvii).

Resources and Dialectics

Let us now get a bit deeper into the features identified above: the particular ontology and epistemology characterising ethnography.

Language is seen as a set of resources, means available to human beings in societies. These resources can be deployed in a variety of circumstances, but when this happens it never happens in a neutral way. Every act of language use is an act that is assessed, weighed, measured socially, in terms of contrasts between this act and others. In fact, language becomes the social and culturally embedded thing it is because of the fact that it is socially and culturally consequential in use. The clearest formulation of this resources view on language can be found in Hymes' essay *Speech and language: on the origins and foundations of inequality among speakers* (1996: Chapter 3). In this strident essay, Hymes differentiates between a linguistic notion of language and an ethnographic notion of speech. Language, Hymes argues, is what linguists have made of it, a concept with little significance for the people who actually use language. Speech is language-in-society, that is, an *active* notion and one that deeply situates language in a web of relations of power, a dynamics of availability and accessibility, a situatedness of single acts vis-à-vis larger social and historical patterns such as genres and traditions. Speech is language in which people have made investments – social, cultural, political, individual-emotional ones. It is also language brought under social control – consequently, language marked by sometimes extreme cleavages and inequalities in repertoires and opportunities.

This has no small consequences to the study of language. For one thing, studying language means studying society, more precisely, it means that all kinds of different meanings, meaning effects, performativities and language functions can and need to be addressed than those current (and accepted) in mainstream linguistics.[5] Second, there is nothing static about this ethnographic view of language. Language appears in reality as performance, as actions performed by people in a social environment. Hence, strict synchrony is impossible as the deployment of linguistic resources is in itself, and step by step as sentences and utterances are constructed, a process. It is this process, and not its linguistic product (statified and reified sentences or utterances) that needs to be understood in ethnography. In order to acquire this understanding, as much attention needs to be given to what is seen from the statified and reified perspective mentioned as 'non-linguistic' matters as needs to be given to strictly 'linguistic' matters. It is at this point that one can understand how ethnography triggered important developments both in general sociology – Bourdieu's work is exemplary in this respect – as well as in kinesics, non-verbal communicative behaviour and indeed social semiosis in general – Goffman, Garfinkel and Goodwin can be mentioned here. From an ethnographic perspective, the distinction between linguistic and non-linguistic is an artificial one since every act of language needs to be situated in wider patterns of human social behaviour, and intricate connections between various aspects of this complex need to be specified: the ethnographic principle of *situatedness*.[6]

It is also relevant to underscore the *critical* potential which ethnography derives from these principles. The constant feedback between communicative actions and social relations involves, as said, reflections on *value* of communicative practices, starting from the observation that not every form of communication is performed or performable in any situation. Society imposes hierarchies and value scales on language, and the looking glass of linguistic practice often provides a magnified image of the workings of powers and the deep structures of inequality in society. It is telling that some of the most critical studies on education have been produced by scholars using an ethnographic perspective (Cook-Gumperz, 1988; Gee, 1996; Heller, 2000; Rampton, 1995). Similarly, it is an interesting exercise to examine the critique formulated from within ethnography against other language scholars involved in the study of language and power. These critiques are not merely critiques of method, they are about the nature of language–power relationships (see Blommaert & Bulcaen, 2000; Blommaert *et al.*, 2001). Moreover, central to this critique is often the notion of language ideologies (Kroskrity, 2000; Woolard *et al.*, 1998): metalinguistic and hence deeply sociocultural ideas of language users about language and communication that not only appear to direct language behaviour and the interpretation of language acts, but also account for folk and official 'rankings' and hierarchies of linguistic varieties.

Object-level (the 'acts' themselves) and metalevel (ideas and interpretations of these acts) cannot be separated in ethnography, for the social value of language is an intrinsic and constituent part of language usage itself; that is, in every act of language people inscribe and mark the social situatedness of these acts and so offer patterns of interpretation to the others. These patterns of interpretation are never fixed, of course, but require acknowledgement and interactional co-construction. So here also, strict synchronicity is impossible, for there is both a processual and a historical dimension to every act of language-in-society (Silverstein & Urban, 1996), and the rankings and hierarchies of language are themselves an area of perpetual debate and conflict (Blommaert, 1999). The social dimension of language is precisely the blending of linguistic and metalinguistic levels in communication: actions proceed with an awareness of how these actions should proceed and can proceed in specific social environments. And to be clear about this point, this means that every language act is intrinsically historical.

This brings us to the epistemological level of ethnography. Knowledge of language facts is processual and historical knowledge, lifting single instances of talk to a level of relevance far higher than just the event. They become indexical of patterns and developments of wider scope and

significance, and these wider dimensions are part of ethnographic interpretation. Static interpretations of context – 'setting', 'speech community'
and so forth – are anathema and to the extent that they occur in ethnographic writing they should be seen as either a rhetorical reduction strategy or worse, as a falsification of the ethnographic endeavour (Fabian,
1983, 1995). Fabian stresses the dynamic process of knowledge gathering
in ethnography, emphasising the fact that ethnographic work also involves
active – very active – involvement from the ethnographer himself (a fact
known from the days of Malinowski and emphasised, for example, by
Edmund Leach, but often overlooked). This provides ethnography with a
peculiar, dynamic and dialectical epistemology in which the *ignorance* of
the knower – the ethnographer – is a crucial point of departure (Fabian,
1995). Consequently, ethnography attributes (and has to attribute) great
importance to the history of what is commonly seen as 'data': the whole
process of gathering and moulding knowledge is part of that knowledge;
knowledge construction *is* knowledge, *the process is the product* (see
Blommaert, 2001, 2004; Ochs, 1979). This is why we will emphasise an
often overlooked function of fieldwork in the remainder of this book: the
fact that fieldwork results in *an archive of research*, which documents the
researcher's own journey through knowledge.

Summarising, language in ethnography is something very different
from what it is in many other branches of the languages sciences, and so is
the status of gathering knowledge. There is no way in which knowledge
of language can be separated from the situatedness of the object at a variety of levels, ranging from microscopic to macroscopic levels of 'context'
and involving, reflexively, the acts of knowledge production by ethnographers themselves.

Ethnography as Counter-hegemony

Walter Benjamin once wrote that the task of historians was to challenge
established and commonly accepted representations of history. History, in
his view, was necessarily critical and counter-hegemonic, and a science
such as history only had a *raison d'être* to the extent that it performed this
role of challenging hegemonies. Exactly the same suggestion can be made
with respect to ethnography: it has the potential and the capacity of challenging established views, not only of language but of symbolic capital in
societies in general. It is capable of constructing a discourse on social uses
of language and social dimensions of meaningful behaviour which differs
strongly from established norms and expectations, indeed takes the concrete functioning of these norms and expectations as starting points for
questioning them, in other words, it takes them as problems rather than as

facts. Central to all of this is the *mapping of resources onto functions*: the way, for instance, in which a standard variety of a language acquires the function of 'medium of education' while a non-standard variety would not. This mapping is socially controlled; it is not a feature of language but one of society. Ethnography becomes critique here: the attributed function of particular resources is often a kind of social imagination, a percolation of social structure into language structure. Ethnography deconstructs this imagination and compares it to observable real forms and functions. It is thus, of necessity, a critical enterprise.

It is also critical in another sense. Whereas in most other approaches, the target of scientific method is *simplification and reduction of complexity*, the target in ethnography is precisely the opposite. Reality is kaleidoscopic, complex and complicated, often a patchwork of overlapping activities. Compare it to a soccer game. Usually, when we watch a soccer game on TV, we are focused on the movement of the ball and on a limited number of players in the area where the ball is. We rarely see all 22 players in the same shot on TV: the lens directs our attention to a subset of the space, the actors and activities. What we miss is the movement of the other players, the way they position themselves in anticipation of what comes next; we also miss the directions they give to one another, by shouting, pointing, pulling faces or making specific gestures. The 22 players perform all sorts of activities simultaneously: while an attacker moves forward with the ball, a winger may run into a favourable position for a particular set-piece play; the central defender can urge his co-defenders to move forward so as to close the gap between forwards and defenders and reduce the space for the opponents when they launch a counter-attack; a midfielder may simultaneously move down to fill in the space left by an attacking defender. And another midfielder may move a bit closer to an attacker from the other side, so as to curtail the latter's opportunities for movement when a counter-attack is launched; he might beckon a fellow midfielder to close the gap he's left by marking the attacker. All the players are constantly monitoring each other, and the coach does the same, shouting instructions to players from the sideline whenever he spots a potential problem. All of this happens at the same time, it is a series of seemingly unrelated – but obviously related – activities, very hard to describe in a linear and coherent narrative *because as an activity it is not linear and coherent* but multiple, layered, chequered and unstable.

A full account of a soccer game should include all of that, for all of it is essential in understanding what happens during the game. Players usually do not arrive at particular positions by accident or luck; they are there because of the complex interlocking activities that produce the game. Ethnography tries to do just that: describe the apparently messy and complex activities that make up social action, not to reduce their complexity but to describe and explain it.[7] This is what makes ethnography a demanding approach: it is not enough (not by a very long shot) to follow a clear, pre-set line of inquiry and the researcher cannot come thundering in with pre-established truths. The procedure is what Hymes (1980: 89) calls 'democratic': 'a mutual relation of interaction and adaptation' between ethnographers and the people they work with, 'a relation that will change both'. That too is counter-hegemonic.

The Ethnographic Argument

We now come to a tricky issue, one that has plagued many researchers facing supervisors and colleagues steeped in a more positivistic tradition of science: representativeness. What exactly do ethnographic data reveal? What sort of relevance do they have for 'society'? How confidently can you make generalisations from your data?

A first and elementary point is this. Ethnography is an *inductive* science, that is: it works from empirical evidence towards theory, not the other way around. This has been mentioned several times already: you *follow* the data, and the data suggest particular theoretical issues. Ethnography, thus, belongs to a range of other scientific disciplines in which induction rather than deduction is the rule – history, law and archaeology are close neighbours. Inductive sciences usually apply what is called the *case method*: a methodology in which one uses case analyses to demonstrate theory. In the words of Lee Shulman (1986: 11):

> A case, properly understood, is not simply the report of an event or incident. To call something a case is to make a theoretical claim – to argue that it is a "case of something", or to argue that it is an instance of a larger class.

Your data *become* cases of such larger categories by applying theoretical models to them; theory is the outcome of a theorisation of your data, you 'theorise them into a case', so to speak. To turn to Shulman again: 'Generalisation does not inhere in the case, but in the conceptual apparatus of the explicator' (1986: 12).

This is an important point: generalisation is perfectly possible, and it depends on the theoretical apparatus that you bring to bear onto your data. Thus, in a situation in which your data are classroom observations about response behaviour by pupils, your data can be framed in, for instance, a Marxist perspective in which social class distinctions are central issues. Your analysis of the data will then focus on features in the data that speak to social class distinctions, and your generalisations will be about such class issues. If you frame your data in a cognitive-psychological theoretical approach, the data will be analysed accordingly and your generalisations will be about cognitive processes you observe in response behaviour.

Such things, of course, do not occur just at the end of your trajectory. You have explored theoretical frameworks prior to starting your field-work, and many of the choices mentioned here have been more or less determined by your particular research preparation and the formulation of your research goals. You usually know beforehand whether you will use a Marxist or a cognitive-psychological framework for your work, and these choices have influenced the design of your fieldwork and, of course, the particular kinds of data you have collected. The important point here is, however, methodological: generalisation is perfectly possible, because your data instantiate a case, and such a case belongs to a larger category of cases. The unique and situated events you have witnessed can and do indeed reveal a lot about the very big things in society.

The case method, as said, is typical for inductive sciences, and especially in legal studies the case method is dominant, also in teaching law. The interesting thing, however, is that it in turn builds upon a much older tradition, which Carlo Ginzburg (1989) calls the *'evidential or conjectural paradigm'*: evidential because it uses (inductive) empirical facts as its point of departure, 'conjectural' because these facts are seen as *probably* meaning this-or-that. The facts generate hypotheses that can then be verified. This paradigm is epitomised by Sherlock Holmes, who was able to deduce more insights from a cigarette butt left in an ashtray than his rival police inspector could by deploying his elaborate (deductive) criminal inves-tigation tactics. But it is also epitomised in clinical medicine, where the surgeon first searches for small symptoms ('clues') that can then be *con-jecturally* related to a larger category – the disease – and then be treated with drugs or other means. Thus the surgeon spots a rash on your arms, a swollen liver and a yellowish colour in your eyes, s/he hypothetically connects this to hepatitis, and then administers drugs to fight hepatitis. The surgeon's hypothesis will be proven correct when the drugs are effective and the symptoms disappear.

Ginzburg finds ancient roots for this paradigm in divination – where the divinator would examine small things in order to predict big things – and he nicely summarises the case:

> the group of disciplines which we have called evidential and conjec-tural (...) are totally unrelated to the scientific criteria that can be

claimed for the Galilean paradigm [in which individual cases do not count – JB & DJ]. In fact, they are highly qualitative disciplines, in which the object is the study of individual cases, situations, and documents, precisely *because they are individual*, and for this reason get results that have an unsuppressible speculative margin; just think of the importance of conjecture (the term itself originates in divination) in medicine or in philology, and in divining. (Ginzburg, 1989: 106)

History, philology, psychoanalysis, archaeology, medicine, law, art history: these are the companions of ethnography in a long and venerable tradition of scientific work. In fact, every truly *social* science falls in this category. Chomsky's linguistics was an attempt to bring the study of language – a social science, evidently – into the orbit of Galilean science. To Chomsky and his followers, linguistics would be a deductive science in which individual *performance* had no place, because individual cases could never invalidate the generalisations made from theory. In other social sciences as well, we have seen how strong the appeal of a deductive Galilean model of science was. The effect has been that the existence, and the validity, of this evidential and conjectural paradigm has been largely forgotten. Yet, it is the methodological basis for generalisation in ethnography, and it is a very firm basis.

Notes

1. The following sections are based on a paper called 'Ethnography as counter-hegemony'; International Literacy Conference, Cape Town 2001, downloadable from http://www.kcl.ac.uk/education/wpull.html.
2. The journal *Ethnography* (launched in 2000) testifies to the impact of ethnography in a wide range of social sciences. An important, and frequent, contributor to the journal was Pierre Bourdieu, operating alongside sociocultural and linguistic anthropologists and microsociologists. Bourdieu's own take on fieldwork and ethnography was exemplified in a special issue of *Ethnography* in 2004 (Wacquant, 2004).
3. Cf. Hymes (1980: 89): 'The earliest work that we recognize as important ethnography has generally the quality of being systematic in the sense of being *comprehensive*'.
4. It may be interesting to point out that this view has percolated contemporary pragmatics. In the introduction to the *Handbook of Pragmatics* (Verschueren, 1995), pragmatics is defined as a functional perspective on language and communication. Verschueren refers, significantly, to Sapir (1929) as a source of inspiration for this view.
5. At a very basic level, this pertains to the assumption that language *has* a function, and that its main purpose is *communication*. Truistic as it now may seem, at various points in the history of the language sciences these points required elaborate arguing.

6. For those who wish to read up on this, Blommaert (2005b) provides an sive discussion of this viewpoint.
7. Erving Goffman's work theorises this complexity, and does so in a highly readable way. See Goffman (1971) for good examples.

Read up on it

Fabian, J. (1983) *Time and the Other: How Anthropology Makes Its Object*. New York: Columbia University Press.

Hymes, D. (1980) *Language in Education: Ethnolinguistic Essays*. Washington, DC: Centre for Applied Linguistics.

Hymes, D. (1986) Models of the interaction of language and social life. In J. Gumperz and D. Hymes (eds) *Directions in Sociolinguistics: The Ethnography of Communication* (2nd edn, pp. 35–71). Oxford: Blackwell.

Chapter 3
The Sequence 1: Prior to Fieldwork

Put simply, fieldwork-based research has three sequential stages:

(1) Prior to fieldwork.
(2) During fieldwork.
(3) After fieldwork.

Roughly, these stages correspond to:

(1) Preparation and documentation.
(2) Fieldwork procedures.
(3) Post-fieldwork analysis and writing.

Of course, each of the stages falls apart into more parts. But whereas the three parts here are necessarily sequential, sub-parts can be overlapping and simultaneous, as we shall see.

Prior to fieldwork, several activities are required, and they can be captured under preparation and documentation. Preparation, of course, starts as soon as one begins research, develops an interest in a particular topic or field, and starts working on a proposal and a work plan. You read considerable volumes of theoretically and methodologically informative work, which is invaluable because it directs your gaze to particular aspects of social reality and sharpens your eyes and ears for particular phenomena and events. That is general preparation, and we need not dwell on it here.

But there will be a decision at a given moment that your research will include fieldwork – ethnographic fieldwork. And this decision has far-reaching consequences, because it places your work on a track which has its own requirements and peculiarities: you now have to subscribe to the general epistemological and methodological principles developed in the previous chapter. You have to adopt an ethnographic *perspective* on your work, and as we saw above, this includes a number of things and excludes a number of others. The result of your research will now *not* be a body of findings which can claim representativeness for a (segment of the) population, it will not be replicable under *identical* circumstances, it will not claim objectivity on grounds of an outsider's position for the researcher, it will not claim to produce 'uncontaminated' evidence, and so on. It will be interpretive research in a situated, real environment, based on inter-action between the researcher and the subject(s), hence, fundamentally *subjective* in nature,[1] aimed at demonstrating complexity, and yielding hypotheses that can be replicated and tested in *similar*, not identical, circumstances. Ethnography produces theoretical statements, not 'facts' nor 'laws'. That does *not* mean that your research will be a game without rules. The rules of ethnographic analysis are as strict and rigorous as those of statistics, and there are more things one can do wrong in ethnographic work than perhaps in any other branch of science.

Your preparation, thus, needs to be rigorous, and it needs to start from a particular way of imagining your object. The object of investigation is always a *uniquely situated reality*: a complex of events which occurs in a totally unique context – time, place, participants, even the weather, quar-rels between the subjects and the ethnographer: you are always working in a series of conditions that can never be repeated. Even if events look completely the same (think of rituals such as religious services), they never are, because they are *different* events happening at another time.[2] So the thing you will investigate will be a particular point in time and space, a microscopic social mechanism: people talking to one another in a village in West Africa, on the 24th of October 2009, a rainy day when Diallo, one of the interlocutors, had a stomach ache which made him flinch every now and then so that the conversation drifted from your favourite topic to that of health and remedies. This is mundane, trivial, seemingly completely irrelevant as a social fact.

It would be, were it not that we conceive of social events as *contextual-ised* and as *ordered*, not random. Whatever people do, they do in a real social environment on which all sorts of forces operate: culture, language, social structure, history, political relations, and so forth. Being a man or a woman, 22 years old or 47 years old, rich or poor – all of that makes a dif-ference in any society, for everywhere we will see that such seemingly self-evident characteristics carry rich cultural meanings and have particu-lar social features. There are societies, for instance, where a 22-year-old person would never consider contradicting a 47-year-old person; there are societies where this can be permissible when the younger one is male and the older one is female, and there are societies where this is the opposite. So here is a central insight: ***uniquely situated events are the crystallisa-tion of various layers of context***, micro-contexts (changeable, accidental, unpredictable contexts, such as foul weather, a power failure during a meal in a restaurant, your recording device refusing duty or the father entering the room just when a conversation with the children had turned into a juicy gossip session) as well as macro-contexts (historical, larger political, social and cultural ones, less changeable and more stable, hence predictable).

To illustrate the difference between these various layers of context: the fact that people speak, for example, Zulu is typically a macro-context. If it is part of their developmental trajectory, they cannot change it, and one will find many people with similar developmental trajectories (coming from the same region, born from parents speaking Zulu, belonging to a Zulu social network) speaking Zulu. A micro-context would be the fact that the Zulu speaker you meet during fieldwork might be particularly articulate, a fantastic storyteller and someone who is really good at establishing contacts on your behalf. The micro-contextual factors operate *locally*: they offer distinctions between Zulu speakers. Macro-contextual factors have wider scope: they offer distinctions between speakers of Zulu and speakers of Xhosa, Ndebele, Swahili and so forth.

Let us, for the sake of clarity, summarise this in a drawing:

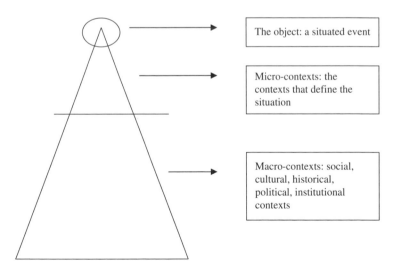

Your object is a needle point in time and space, and it can only gain relevance when it is adequately contextualised in micro- and macro-contexts. This contextualisation explains why your object has the features it has and why it lacks others; it also allows you to see, in microscopic events, effects of macroscopic structures, phenomena and processes. When someone says 'yes sir', this is a microscopic, almost trivial thing. Context tells us, however, that this innocuous formula draws on enduring systems of power and authority in our society, as well as on gender roles and structures, ideologies of politeness and etiquette. The microscopic, trivial instance of using it now becomes something far richer: we see that the user of the phrase summarises a world of (macro-contextual) social rules and conventions in his/her innocuous, routinised utterance, and submits to it. He/she displays 'conventional' behaviour, that is, behaviour that exudes the dominant social structures and expectations. The event in itself does not tell us that; the contextualisation of the event does that.

The main task during your fieldwork preparation is, thus, *to understand and study the possible contexts in which your object will occur*, micro as well as macro. This will expand the range of recognisable things – not everything will be totally strange and unexpected – and lower the risk of asking the wrong questions and behaving totally out of order. It *lowers* these risks, but does not *eliminate* them, of course. If you intend to do fieldwork in a primary school in a country called Absurdistan, for instance, it is good to know

(1) That there *are* in effect such schools in Absurdistan.
(2) Some basic and general things about how such schools operate (do they have daily and full-day sessions, for instance? How large are the classes? Are they gender-separated? What is the language of instruction?).
(3) Whether there are regional divisions, or urban–rural divisions, that could be important foci of research (you cannot draw conclusions about 'education in Absurdistan' if there are very deep differences between education in different parts of the country – in Africa it is, for instance, good to keep in mind that outside the cities, many parts of many countries do not have any education provision to speak of).
(4) Some general things about the legal provisions for such schools, and about their institutional structure. (E.g. Are all schools state-controlled or is there a division between public and private schools? Is there a 'secondary' market for education – private tutoring, evening schools, commercial internet or correspondence courses, etc.?)
(5) General information about Absurdistan, its history, social structure, politics, major languages, media and so forth.
(6) The tradition of scholarship on education in Absurdistan, the major centres for research, and the major researchers, policy makers and authority figures in the field.

Therefore your preparation is about getting to understand what Bourdieu called the 'field' of education in Absurdistan: the whole complex of surrounding conditions in which a single school becomes part of a system and a society, including historical, social, cultural, linguistic, political backgrounds. It is an attempt at constructing 'normal', expectable and presupposable patterns, things you can reasonably expect to meet in the field. All these things matter; researching them pays off. If you would have overlooked point (1) above, for instance, you could find yourself in the embarrassing situation of not having a field to do fieldwork in. Having spent substantial sums of money and even more substantial amounts of time, we would prudently qualify this as a serious problem (certainly if you are scheduled to complete your doctorate in the next 16 months . . .).

That is obvious, but even inquiries into (5), for instance, may provide immediate answers for other parts. Imagine that Absurdistan would be a People's Republic with a rather radical communist government; that would immediately trigger an expectation that the education system in Absurdistan would be fully state-controlled. Your research would then by definition focus on work in state-controlled schools, working (probably) with a unified curriculum and employing teachers who have had a very similar training. If, now, you discover the existence of a flourishing but clandestine private education market during your fieldwork in Absurdistan, this insight gains importance, for one can expect this to be at odds with the policy provisions and dominant ideology of the country. It would mean that people perceive the formal education system as deficient, or realise that what they learn in schools is not enough for the kinds of social trajectories they have in mind, or even that there is a lot of dissent in the country, and that education is a focal area in organising this dissent. You may, then, have found the existence of two parallel and complimentary systems of education, one formal and another commercial, around which people organise different views, expectations and patterns of performance. This, of course, would be a major finding, because 'education in Absurdistan' now becomes a highly complex thing, and your observations in official schools should be balanced against observations elsewhere.

Take another example. You find out that Absurdistan was a communist People's Republic until three years ago, when the regime changed to a capitalist multiparty system with strong ties to the United States and the EU. These new partners have since become very active in the field of development support, and the education system has been overhauled by American and European technical advisors. You now know that you will in all likelihood encounter a very complex and perhaps paradox-ridden education field, in which teachers trained to be good communists have to induce their pupils into the virtues of pro-Western capitalism (but might not know very well how to do that), in which people would constantly compare the 'old' versus the 'new' education system, and in which you would probably see a rapidly increasing class division between private, urban elite schools and old-style public schools. Your research would then, in all likelihood, be compelled to address these features of transition and contradiction.

A lot of this documentary research needs to be done prior to departing for the field. Some parts of it, however, may only be possible over there. You might need access to specific archives, for instance, or some things can only be found out by going to the local Ministry of Education and asking people there. As said, it is important, because it leads to, and helps you in, more practical aspects of preparation. For instance, and very importantly, it can help you decide whether the topic you had in mind is

(1) *Worth researching*: Is it big enough as a topic, is it promising in terms of findings, are there specific documentary/empirical and theoretical issues that may be addressed through fieldwork there?

(2) *Researchable*: This is very important: many topics are very much worth researching, but practically, legally or otherwise unresearchable. There may be ethical restrictions, legal and political ones (authorities not releasing crucial information, or not granting research permits for particular forms and topics of research), material ones (fieldwork would be too expensive or would require a massive research infra-structure) or others. Research in a war zone, for instance, is as good as impossible, even if the situation in that region cries for thorough and sustained research and even if people there would be genuinely helped by your work. The same goes for many 'slum' environments around the world: they are extraordinarily fascinating places and we absolutely need a clear and detailed understanding of life in such environments, but the conditions for research are such that research-ers could expose themselves to serious danger even entering the area. There are also people who might put you in grave danger when you decide to do research with and on them – think of gangs or rebel movements.[3] Researchability is a major decision you need to make during the preparation phase, and thorough preparatory research is essential in making it.

In addition, preparatory research of course helps you in deciding issues such as the general target(s) of your research, the patterns of work you will develop – observations, interviews, single-site or multiple-site research, etc. – the number and kinds of informants you would probably need in order to get your findings, the amount of administrative procedure you need to follow (visa requirements, research permits, ethical clearance, local reporting and so on). It helps you select the schools you will work in, establish first contacts with local people in schools and communities, find out a bit about what goes on there prior to your arrival, and establish interaction with local researchers or institutes. Good preparation helps you to be *realistic* in all of this.

Part of this realism, and unfortunately often overlooked, is *to have a Plan B*. Be aware of the fact that every aspect of fieldwork can go completely wrong, even if it is based on the most meticulously prepared and detailed plan. You are working in a real social environment and with real people. The informants you had contacted prior to your fieldwork may no longer be there, may now bluntly refuse cooperation or demand huge sums of money in return. The people you wanted (and needed) to interview refuse to be interviewed or keep postponing the appointments to do the interviews. The archive material you absolutely need is not there or not accessible. Or, you may fall out with your collaborators in the field, people may start turning their backs on you. Or, your video recorder refuses duty from day one, and there is no way in which you can get a new one – while a crucial part of your research ought to be based on video data. Or, you get involved in a nasty traffic accident and get a bad neck injury requiring weeks of hospitalisation and rehabilitation. All of these things have happened in our experience as fieldworkers and fieldwork supervisors. There you go.

It is thus very wise to think of, and develop, a research plan that can still be carried through even if all goes wrong. If your research is dependent on one major type of data – say video recordings of classroom practices – or on particular formats of work such as interviewing, close work with informants, etc. you must think of something that can be researched from other types of data and through other means (a policy study, an analysis of teaching materials or of pupils' notebooks, an inquiry into adjacent fields such as the labour market or teacher training programmes). This will require different topics, aims, procedures. That is not an easy job, but as we shall see in the next section, it is best to put it in your bag because work in the field can be very unpredictable.

Notes

1. Bourdieu teaches us – importantly – that the distinction between 'objective' and 'subjective' is a false one: the subjective is the basis of any form of

'objectivity'. As mentioned earlier, his own work was consistently ethnographic in perspective, even if (like *Distinction*) it looked aridly factual and statistical. Read his *Logic of Practice* (1990; see also Blommaert, 2005a).

2. One of the frequent complaints of beginning fieldworkers is that 'it's always the same thing'. This means, of course, that one is looking at *routines* and *rituals*: things that are tremendously important in every social environment, and that derive part of their importance *exactly* from being 'always the same thing'.

3. A research student working in East Africa during the first Gulf War once called Jan with a moral dilemma. His informant had brought back an accidental tape recording of a conversation between two men who discussed the sale of a couple of kilos of enriched uranium. These were brilliant data, of course, as lots of jargon was used. But thinking that perhaps these people would not be overly pleased if they found out that their chat had been recorded and might contemplate unpleasant forms of revenge, we declared this topic unresearchable.

Chapter 4

The Sequence 2: In the Field

Fieldwork itself is humanly demanding, as a fieldworker will need to give proof of all the good qualities in life: patience, endurance, stamina, perseverance, flexibility, adaptability, empathy, tolerance, the willingness to lose a battle in order to win a war, creativity, humour and wit, diplomacy, and being happy about very small achievements. Put that in a job advertisement and you will never find a suitable candidate.

Chaos

Since most of us are only human, fieldwork is often a period of deep frustration, disappointment and confusion, sometimes even of bitter tears. The main frustration is due to the widespread perception and experience that fieldwork is *chaotic*. It can contain long periods in which nothing seems to happen, and then suddenly all sorts of things co-occur rapidly and seemingly without structure or patterns, certainly not with the clear structure and patterns one had picked up from the literature. (At these moments of acceleration, you discover that you forgot your tape recorder of course.) People contradict each other, and just when you think you found the key to the whole thing, the whole thing changes again. The plan has to be revised over and over again, as certain administrative procedures take forever and some of your key informants are on leave or have better things to do. Above all, the topic you had so nicely sketched in your research proposal turns out to be either very different than what you expected, or to be more than one topic and a cluster of things that need to be investigated step by step in ways you had not anticipated.

It was certainly chaotic when Dong Jie set off for her fieldwork in Beijing migrant schools.[1] The fieldwork was well-prepared: she had read tons of literature around the topic, decided on the theoretical frame, gone through the research plan with colleagues and friends, built up contacts that would have ideal access to the fieldwork sites. She even corresponded with a couple of key researchers in this field for half a year prior to the fieldwork. As soon as she landed in the field, however, she discovered that fieldwork was full of surprises, not always pleasant ones. First, the contact person who was keen to introduce Dong Jie to one of the migrant schools was away for a research project in a remote village and no one had any idea when she would be back to Beijing.

Thus as soon as the fieldwork started Dong Jie had to revise the research plan and adopt new strategies: she mobilised everyone she knew to look for accessible migrant schools and she conducted a carpet-searching for such schools. Luckily several migrant schools were found in the area and she decided to knock on the schoolmasters' doors. According to her plan, teaching in a migrant school would be an ideal pattern for the research as teaching would enable her to interact with the pupils and would in turn yield deeper understanding of the population. 'To be a teacher here? Yes of course you are welcome. But you have to teach from 7AM to 5PM, Monday to Saturday for at least one year and we require school residence'. These were impossible commitments for Dong Jie to make as she had other duties to perform in the meantime.

Once again, she had to be flexible and to devise new strategy. This time she decided to negotiate with the schoolmasters about her access to their schools for research and see what the schools wanted in return. 'Research? No, we don't accept any researcher except you have a recommendation from the LEA'. If this was what Dong Jie needed, she was determined to get one. She approached the LEA and presented her research plan. 'Yes it is an interesting research. We will consider it'. Unfortunately, the consideration took very long. A couple of months passed in the wait-and-search mode, and it was increasingly frustrating to see so little progress. Nobody could foresee at that moment that Dong Jie would be on 'a rollercoaster of luck' and running between schools in the second half of the fieldwork.

Chaos is the normal state of things. It is nothing to worry about. Remember what we set out to do: to describe and analyse *complexity*, not to simplify a complex social event into neat tables and lines. So we should not be surprised if the social events we observe are not linear, not perfectly logical, not clearly sequential, not dominated by rational decisions and so on: life is not like that. Try to describe *everything* you do when you perform a single activity such as crossing a busy street – every sensory and bodily movement, and every thought and decision – and you know what we are talking about: human behaviour is stunningly complex. But there is an interesting twist: the perception of chaos is gradually replaced by one of order, and this has to do with the learning process of fieldwork. *The more we get to understand the contexts of events, the less we experience such events as chaotic*. If we return to the example of crossing a street: for most people this would be a single action – you simply cross the street – and the reason is that we've done it thousands of times and have developed routinised procedures for it, procedures we no longer perceive as part of the activity, but just as a canvas, a neutral background to the activity itself. *Of course* we look carefully left and right before we decide to cross, *of course* we adjust our walking speed to that of approaching vehicles, and *of course* we will step back when a car is approaching too fast or is already too close to us. *How else could we cross the street?* So what is essentially a tremendously complicated bundle of activities is now seen as one logically structured, almost automatic activity of extreme simplicity. And if crossing a street is already a complex thing, one can imagine what degree of complexity a social network must have; yet all of us move through various such networks on a daily basis and seem not to encounter major problems doing so. Chaos becomes order because we got used to the chaos.

Fieldwork has to start from the assumption that what is observed will be chaotic. Also, we need to understand that *a priori*, we never know the boundaries of events. We never know exactly in advance what we will need to include in our observations and what not. We can set out to investigate literacy practices and quickly discover that we first need to investigate oral proficiency levels among pupils, for instance. This will determine a lot of what follows, as we shall see.

The Learning Process

Fieldwork is traditionally seen as 'data collection'. This is true to some extent. Of course you should return from the field loaded with bags full of 'data': raw and half-processed materials that reflect and document the realities in the field. But fieldwork should not just be reduced to data collection, because essentially it is *a learning process*. The researcher almost by definition arrives as an outsider: someone who is not part of the social environment in which s/he will do research, has limited knowledge of the people, the normal patterns of everyday conduct, the climate and culture of the place. The preparation has ideally provided some knowledge, but as we know, social environments drive on a lot of tacit understanding, on unspoken routines and conventions, on shared experiences and outlooks – and none of that belongs to the researcher's background. The fieldworker gradually learns these tacit codes, and gradually moves from the margins of the social environment to a more central position.

There can be a degree of overlap, of course, when the researcher does have experience in that field. In educational research, for instance, researchers can have a long and rich experience as teachers, and so be familiar with the life world and the organisation of an educational environment. But even so, when that teacher turns into a researcher s/he stops being a teacher. For one thing, when you do fieldwork you don't enter the school to teach but to do research. A lot of what is understood and taken for granted from the perspective of the teacher needs to be called into question by the researcher. Thus, there is a long history of difficult relationships in 'native ethnography' as it is called: the colleagues you observe may be surprised, even upset by the reflections and comments you make as a researcher, and the researcher may be annoyed by the fact that erstwhile close colleagues now see him/her as an intruder and adapt their behaviour accordingly. The fact that you are familiar with the rules of a place does not necessarily work for your benefit: as a researcher you almost necessarily *transgress* these rules – you ask silly questions, you pry on people's activities, you stand where you are not supposed to stand, you disturb normal routines – and such transgressions can be held against you precisely because the others know that you are familiar with the rules. The outsider has the advantage of innocence (provided this is granted to him/her). Early in your fieldwork, you can find that people are very tolerant towards your deviant behaviour; the longer you stick around, however, the more they may expect you to adjust to expected behaviour. Your initial ignorance can be a useful fieldwork instrument, but it rarely lasts.

Being an outsider, to be sure, does not mean that you are non-existent and of no consequence to what goes on. When a researcher enters a classroom, the whole classroom changes, and a lot of what the researcher will witness are reactions, adjustments and adaptations to this change. As a fieldworker, you never belong 'naturally' or 'normally' to the field you investigate, you are always a foreign body which causes ripples on the surface of smooth routinised processes. *There is always an observer's effect*, and it is essential to realise that: you are never observing an event as if you were not there. You are there, and that makes it a different event.

> The observer's effect was obvious at the beginning of Dong Jie's fieldwork. After several months' searching, she ended up with a primary school, of which the schoolmaster was interested in the research – she asked Dong Jie to set up and to lead a research team of four teachers and the schoolmaster herself, and insisted that the research team

should observe the class with Dong Jie. You can imagine how the class would look like with six people sitting at the back and watching: the teachers were nervous, students quiet, classes rehearsed! In the first few days the observation was fruitless – what they observed was miles away from its usual state. The four teacher researchers quickly dropped out because they were busy with their own teaching, but the schoolmaster was in class with Dong Jie for several weeks. This was the last thing Dong Jie expected in the fieldwork – teachers and pupils were nervous of the schoolmaster's presence and their behaviours were adapted to her preference. In Dong Jie's plan, she would chat with the teachers and pupils during breaks, but the schoolmaster often invited Dong Jie to her office for a cup of tea (which was very kind of her but did no good to the fieldwork). There was little Dong Jie could do, except privately hoping that the schoolmaster suddenly became very busy with her routine work. Fortunately the schoolmaster stopped the class observation about a month later, and by then the teachers and pupils had become familiar with Dong Jie.

There are different stages and degrees to this effect. When you sit in a classroom for the 25th day in a row, chances are that the others have long started seeing you as part of the décor and take no notice of you anymore. The observer's effect is significant in the early stages of fieldwork and may diminish as fieldwork goes on. As to degrees, it is clear that if you stuff the classroom with video cameras and audio-equipment, or move around with a camera continually pointed at the teacher's face, chances are that you will be perceived to be seriously disrupting. Hanging a microphone around a teacher's neck may make him/her feel quite uncomfortable, as s/he will have a tendency to 'talk to the mike' and not to the class.[2] Talking to teachers and pupils during breaks, on the other hand, is obviously less of a distortion of set practices.

The learning process is thus mutual: the others learn about you, get used to your presence and start understanding what you are after; you start to get accustomed to the normal ways of organising their activities and the patterns such activities take, you start knowing the teachers and their reputations (and you start forming an opinion about them), as well as the pupils – the 'good' and 'bad' ones, the 'nerds' and the 'cool' ones – the school culture, the neighbourhood, the institutional context in which the school operates. This mutual learning process becomes the 'common ground' between researchers and subjects, the thing that enables particular forms of interaction to take place and particular kinds of knowledge to travel between the two parties. ***The things we call 'data' gain*** *profile and relevance in relation to this more general learning process.* And to these data we now turn. We will address three clusters of activities: (1) observation and fieldnotes; (2) interviewing and what we shall for the sake of convenience call (3) the collection of rubbish.

Observation and Fieldnotes

You observe all the time. Whenever your eyes and ears are open and you are in a clear state of mind, you register things that strike you. In everyday life we don't have a word for this (we just do it); in fieldwork we call this 'observation'. And the rule is: you start by observing *everything* and gradually start focusing on *specific targets*. The main instruments for that are your eyes, your ears, your mouth and your notebook, and you can use visual and other recording devices in support of that.

Observing 'everything'

Saying that you observe 'everything' is not very helpful of course. You can only watch if you know where to look, and that depends on understanding, where you are and what you're doing there – here is the issue of preparation again. But the point is that the beginning phase of fieldwork is a phase of finding your way around a particular place, registering faces and voices, discovering itineraries to get from one place to another (and for those working in educational environments, schools can be awfully complex spaces, to be sure). You have a particular topic in mind – say, observing the classroom literacy practices in the third grade – and your attention will quickly go in that direction. But pending full focus on these bits, *you observe indiscriminately in an attempt to get an overall image.* You try to see all the teachers and staff, discover the whole of the school, make walks in the neighbourhood so as to know and understand where the pupils come from, and try to get a more or less precise idea of what goes on there. Make sure you have this general image before you actually move in to your focal site, the third grade classroom. It will help you grasp what goes on there, as the school is obviously a context of major importance for the class. You may discover that the third grade teacher has an excellent reputation among his colleagues; everyone speaks highly about him. But soon after that, you may discover that his reputation is mainly built on his rigorous insistence on strict discipline, that he is known for being severe on underachievers, and that his class actually has a very high failure and drop-out rate.

Knowing such things creates, as said earlier, *patterns of expectation*: when you now enter his classroom you know more or less what you will encounter there. You can start zooming in on particular aspects of that now: the struggle of the underachievers, the way in which the teacher makes judgement calls about who does well and who doesn't, the criteria he appears to use for that (e.g. 'clean' and aesthetically elaborated writing as opposed to correct but rather sloppy writing) and the way in which his system of discipline has effects on the pupils' behaviour (e.g. how some try to ingratiate themselves with him by volunteering for housekeeping tasks, others rather remain silent than give a wrong answer . . .). You also find out that some of the most obedient and servile pupils in class are vitriolic and rebellious about the teacher during the break, and that some of the silent ones in class are highly vocal and articulate during breaks. All of these small things now start making sense as parts of a broader pattern, the particular learning regime created by the teacher's focus on discipline and achievement. Your search around the school has also yielded another insight: the teacher has a good reputation among his peers because the school has a poor reputation, and he is seen as one of the teachers who 'gets results', makes no compromises with weaker pupils, and maintains a regime of learning that matches that of 'better' schools. Small things start becoming meaningful in relation to bigger things, and you begin to see how these bigger things have their grounding in small things. You start seeing how the events you observe form part of a *system*.

Finding out such things demands, as you now can see, **observation at various levels, different times and places** – the classroom during class periods, the breaks, the school more generally, the staff common room, and so on. And it also (even more importantly) demands **making connections** between bits of information gathered at these different levels, times and places – this is the work of *contextualisation*: things you find here need to be connected to things found elsewhere in attempts to establish contextual connections ('this is an effect of that', 'this belongs to the same category as that', 'this can only be understood in relation to that' . . .).

> Dong Jie came across a teacher at the school – he was one of the only two male teachers there. He enjoyed a reputation of being kind, easy-going, and ready to help among his colleagues. Dong Jie felt the same at the beginning until she found his class (drawing class) was often either curiously silent or easily out of control. Dong Jie also noticed a girl who was considered a 'good' student by most other teachers was rather undisciplined in his class. The pupils later told Dong Jie that the pupils did not like the drawing teacher because he used physical punishments to discipline them. They had reported this to other teachers, as physical discipline is a serious breach of teaching code in China (especially in Beijing), but nothing was changed. This is rather

puzzling: why his reputation among teachers and that among pupils were so contradictory, and why no action was taken against his behaviour.

To understand this, we have to posit the case in the context at different levels: at a personal level, the drawing teacher used to teach in a secondary school and was calmer while dealing with adults but might easily lose his temper with children; at a school level, the primary school was seriously imbalanced in term of teachers' male/female ratio and therefore needed him; at a country level, education reform encourages self-autonomy and individuality among pupils whereas practitioners (also the drawing teacher at this school) complain that the new approaches are not as effective as the traditional ones in disciplining pupils, given the particular characteristics of Chinese children – most of whom are the only child of their families and can be self-centred and difficult to discipline.

It's like making a big jigsaw puzzle, and you will find yourself developing numerous hypotheses about such connections and making numerous attempts before the puzzle fits.

Making recordings

Part of the observation process (but as we have seen, by no means *all* of the observation process) consists of making recordings: audio, video and/ or visual recordings; we should add 'collecting' as well: collecting copies of pupils' notebooks or coursework, or of tests you developed and administered; collecting samples of the teaching materials used by the teacher, and so on.

The finality of recordings is dual. On the one hand, these recordings provide you with the 'raw data' that will eventually substantiate your analysis as 'evidence' and 'examples'. They will be the bits of first-hand information that will be crucial in making your account of events stick academically. So your recordings have an important function *after the fieldwork*, and we'll come back to it later. On the other hand, recordings also have important functions *during fieldwork*. They provide you with *an archive of your own research*. Recordings made in the beginning of fieldwork will be different from recordings made at a more advanced stage of your work, the reason being that your gaze has shifted towards more specific topics and events. Consequently, whereas in the initial stages you would be highly satisfied when you made a long audio recording of a whole class period, including all the not-so-relevant bits, such recordings would be seen as less than satisfactory later on in the game. The collection of recordings, in that sense, documents your own progression through the learning process, it testifies to the way in which you yourself have become familiar with what goes on there.

This is very important, because one of the features of the learning process is that you tend to forget where you came from. Things that strike you as strange and remarkable in the beginning cease to do that soon after, and after some time all kinds of initially remarkable things are taken for granted because they have become part of your own outlook on things. Yet, your initial ignorance and amazement are crucial: they provide the beginning stages of *ethnographic understanding*, and the accumulation of knowledge during fieldwork is exactly the process you need to document and establish. The archive of your fieldwork ideally contains *everything you need to reconstruct your itinerary from being an outsider to being a knowing member of a community*, someone who now can analyse confidently what went on.

> Upon going through Dong Jie's audio recordings again, we find that her early recordings are either entire class sessions or hours of long and unstructured interviews. These recordings remind us of how curious she was at the beginning – the teaching was organised rather differently from what she expected and the pupils were a lot more active and vocal than Dong Jie's generation. A couple of weeks later everything became natural and the length of her recordings was reduced to between ten and twenty minutes. The topics in the interviews were narrowed down to just a few: comments on migrant pupils' accents, the friends they made in schools, and parents' expectations of their academic career.

As a fieldworker you often travel from an innocent outsider to a knowledgeable member of the field, and you therefore need a careful record of that trajectory – we will come back to that below when we discuss fieldnotes.

Photographs can be an important help in the creation of your own archive. There too, you will find yourself making different pictures in the beginning and towards the end of your fieldwork. In the beginning, you will try to capture documentary things, things that assist you in finding your way around. Gradually, the photographs will become 'data': snapshots of children writing, of the teacher lecturing – things you perhaps think can be useful as illustrations in your dissertation and/or in publications or presentations afterwards. You will start taking pictures of pages from the notebooks or textbooks used in class, of the blackboard, of drawings made by pupils, of notices displayed in the school; etc. Afterwards, all of these images will be tremendously helpful in reminding

Figure 4.1 Pupils watching a performance (taken in the beginning of Dong Jie's fieldwork)

you of what places, moments and people were like. Looking at a picture will trigger a vivid memory of the moment when you took it; it will trigger the recollection of an anecdote that might exactly be the thing you need in a particular place in your analytical argument (see Figures 4.1 and 4.2).

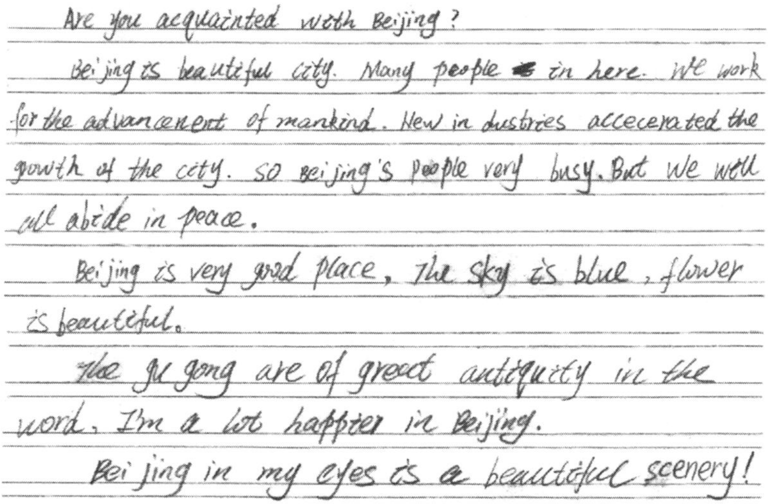

Are you acquainted with Beijing?

Beijing is beautiful city. Many people in here. We work for the advancement of mankind. New industries accecerated the growth of the city. so Beijing's people very busy. But we will all abide in peace.

Beijing is very good place, The sky is blue, flower is beautiful.

The gu gong are of great antiquity in the word. I'm a lot happier in Beijing.

Bei jing in my eyes is a beautiful scenery!

Figure 4.2 A pupil's homework, taken in the second month

Let's now return to the issue of recordings. Usually, making recordings is considered to be an intrusive measure. In fact, it is, of course, because what you do is to capture something which normally remains 'on the spot', and 'export' it, so to speak, to other times and places. Words spoken by someone without further thoughts can become crucial building blocks in someone else's academic argument; they can find their way into published papers, and they may be accompanied by critical remarks about the words and the one who uttered them. Innocent utterances may become politically sensitive ones due to interventions from the researcher. Recordings are always sensitive materials, things that people may experience as threatening.

Normally, therefore, people will impose *conditions on recording*. They will insist that you obtain official permission for making recordings (from the principal, the teacher, the pupils' guardians, sometimes the higher authorities as well), they may insist that you leave a copy of the recordings with them or that your recordings will be destroyed after the completion of your research, and so on. They might also request that you do not record certain things, or that you restrict your recording to specific times and occasions ('not now' is a frequently heard answer to a request for making recordings).

You submit to these conditions of course, but you should make sure that people understand, and agree to, two things very clearly:

(1) That your recordings will be used exclusively for academic purposes, but that they are essential for your academic purposes. In other words: it is no use if they allow you to make recordings but insist on the destruction of your recordings immediately after the completion of research. These data should be granted a life beyond the PhD, since they are *scientific* materials that will only be treated scientifically.[3] Your own integrity is at play here: you will have to convince people of your good intentions. You can commit this to paper in a protocol, you can refer to existing ethical guidelines to which you subscribe and against which your conduct can be measured, and you can invoke higher authorities by producing written assurances from your supervisors or research officers.

(2) That the scientific use of these recordings will involve a process of modification of these data, such that the personal interests of the recorded individuals are protected: all names will be changed, faces may be made unrecognisable, people will be consulted in cases of doubt. This too can be committed to paper in a protocol. Sometimes the effects of this are cumbersome. Imagine video data in which

precisely the direction of the pupils' gaze is essential to your analysis. Ethically, you should cover the eyes of the children visible on the video stills, which is rather awkward if your analysis is about their gaze. A way out is to make a print of the stills, put them on a lighted glass plate, put a blank sheet on top of it and make a drawing of the picture. This effectively anonymises the children, while it affords you enough detail to state your case about gaze direction.

Since recording is considered sensitive and intrusive, *don't make your recording sessions a turkey shoot*. Don't start recording anything and all the time; make arrangements and appointments, prepare your recording sessions well, and record things you believe will be maximally salient and informative. Better return with a limited collection of high-quality recordings than with a pile of recordings of which only a small fraction will deserve further attention. Make sure your recording devices are in good working order – try them and double check!

> Once a teacher became very open (which was very rare) and telling Dong Jie her about her insight on her migrant pupils' education and commented on their language use, which was the exact data Dong Jie wanted; to Dong Jie's great disappointment, her digital voice recorder ran out of battery, because it was switched on by mistake in her pocket on the way to the school until it ran out. She of course made fieldnotes immediately afterwards, but it wouldn't be as good as a recorded interview, as the teacher herself had a strong Beijing accent and she mimicked her pupils accents and these interesting data could only be reconstructed by voice recording.

Confirm that your recording devices work, and put them in such spots that they capture adequate quality data without disturbing the normal order of the setting too much. If you put a big microphone on the teacher's desk in such a way that s/he cannot put his/her papers there, that is usually not a good idea.[4] As for the placing of your recording devices: it is an old tradition to focus on the teacher in classroom research, but one must realise that a classroom (and this counts by extension for almost any social environment) is *polycentric*, it has more than one focal point. The pupils are also a 'centre', and ideally, your recordings would reflect what goes on in relation to the different centres. You want to capture the teacher's voice as well as that of the pupils, and if the principal walks in or a piece of music is played during a class period, you also want this to be recognisable from your recordings. That means that you use a wide-scope microphone (not a 'pointer', a microphone that captures sounds from one direction only) and put it in such a position that everything you want to record can be recorded. But remember: a recording is *never* comprehensive, there will always be 'blind spots' – a problem which is more outspoken with video than with audio recordings.

> Listening to Dong Jie's early class session recordings when the schoolmaster was always present, you might consider the classes well organised, the teachers confident, and pupils quickly responding to questions. Dong Jie's fieldnotes, however, reveal how tense the teachers looked, and how straight the students sat: enough to realise that the class sessions were not in their natural state and were rehearsed, and the recordings are misleading without the company of fieldnotes.

Therefore, if you are physically present during the recording session, *make notes* of what you see and hear; that creates a secondary, back-up record of the session, and it can fill important blanks when you start analysing the recorded materials (e.g. it is often hard to identify who speaks from a recording, especially when there are group discussions or multilateral interactions going on; your notes can then tell you who participated, what they said and so on).

Remove your equipment immediately after the session and check the quality of the recording. If the circumstances allow that, *listen to the whole recording as soon as possible after the recording session, and make notes while you listen.* Do not postpone this: your memory of faces, voices and particular events will fade quickly, and whereas you will still be able to recognise a voice as that of a particular pupil a few hours after the recording, you won't be able to do that a few weeks later.

> As Dong Jie's fieldwork became increasingly demanding, especially when she was allowed access to another school, she didn't manage to go through recordings for a couple of weeks until she made an appointment for a follow-up interview and realised that she needed to listen to the first interview (which was a group interview) again. It was a researcher's nightmare to search a twenty minute long recording in a collection of 20 hours of recordings; what was more disturbing was that she couldn't make up her mind which one of the pupils was the interviewee she was looking for. At least, this worked as a warning for Dong Jie to tide up and label the recordings before it piled up to 30 hours or 40 hours.

You of course keep a detailed *catalogue* of your recordings. You can do this in your fieldnotes or in a separate document. In that catalogue, you give every recording an 'identity tag': a number or a code, along with the date, time, place of recording, the participants, and either a brief description of the contents or a number of key words that distinguish that particular recording. This will be of immense help afterwards when you want to dig out particular parts of your corpus for purposes of transcription and analysis.

We have emphasised the notion of an *archive* of your research at various places already. What you collect during fieldwork are building blocks for an archive that documents your work and your own gradual process of learning and understanding. You construct this archive *for yourself*, not for your supervisors or your doctoral committee, and you will need it for any further step in the process of research. It is all about building a disciplined and structured recollection of the events you observed. This will become even more prominent when we discuss fieldnotes.

Fieldnotes

Fieldnotes are a variant of a very old genre: the diary. In anthropology, their value is controversial because fieldnotes often contradict the end result of ethnography – books or articles. The publication of Bronislaw Malinowski's fieldwork diaries called into question a lot of what he had written in his classic ethnographic works. Here was a man who expressed extreme confusion, boredom, anger, racial superiority even about the people whose culture he afterwards described in flattering and affectionate terms. The confusion and emotional orientations in the fieldnotes eventually make way for the aesthetics and genre requirements of academic prose, and contradictions or paradoxes there become coherent and linear features, obscure pieces become symbolic, and what looked like a half-finished jigsaw puzzle now becomes a fine painting.

We attach great importance to fieldnotes, if for nothing else because we still use and re-use our own field notebooks, some of which, in Jan's case, are now over two decades old.[5] They still provide us with invaluable information, not only about *what* we witnessed in the field, but even more importantly about *how* we witnessed it – amazed, outraged, amused, factual and neutral, puzzled, curious, not understanding, confident about our own interpretations. They still tell us a story about *an epistemic process*: the way in which we tried to make new information understandable for ourselves, using our own interpretive frames, concepts and categories, and gradually shifting into new frames, making connections between earlier and current events, finding our way in the local order of things.

That is the main function of fieldnotes: along with the other materials we discussed here, they are crucial in building the archive of your research. They will be, and will remain, your material memory of field-work, of the things you learned and how you learned them. Hence, you must be meticulous about them: make a habit – a *disciplined* habit, which not even a night out with friends can break – of writing entries in them, and make your entries comprehensive and detailed. This can be tough: after a very long day in which all went wrong, a bottle of beer and your bed may have a far stronger appeal than an additional hour behind your desk penning down your day's notes. But you *have* to do it, the reward for such hardship will come later, when you have forgotten events and details and when your notes remind you of important things you were about to overlook.

> An example came from Dong Jie's fieldnotes: after visiting many private migrant schools, Dong Jie was puzzled with a phenomenon the schools shared: they all had their school gates tightly locked (which posed big problem for her to get in touch with anyone inside), whereas most public schools kept their gates open. Why? All of them smiled but nobody gave any answer. Only when going through her earliest fieldnotes Dong Jie recalled that an informant once said some-thing like a child was kidnapped from a nearby private migrant school. So this makes sense: the private migrant schools were more vulnerable than public schools because they were not officially recog-nised in the first place; they therefore had to be more concerned with security issues especially when there was news about child kidnap-ping; they were reluctant to tell this to Dong Jie (as a researcher) because this was not a piece of comforting news and might discour-age their potential pupils as well as their parents. Moreover, most private migrant schools were operating on a limited budget so that they couldn't afford hiring a security guard, which was a common practice of public schools.

Do not attempt to be Cartesian in your fieldnotes: you can afford your-self to be subjective and impressionistic, emotional or poetic. Use the most appropriate way of expressing what you want to express, do not write for an audience, and do not feel constrained by any external pressure: your fieldnotes are private documents, and you will be the only one to decide what you will release from them. You can use them for anything apart from their 'diary' function: for cataloguing the materials you have col-lected, for preliminary transcripts and analyses, for notes made during recording sessions, for anecdotes or accounts of things you saw on TV – their use is unrestricted as long as you make it a repository of knowledge gathered in a learning process. If you keep that final function well in mind, your notes will be rich and useful, way beyond the immediate purpose they serve.

> The idea of writing up fieldnotes for her supervisors was very real for Dong Jie in the initial stage of her fieldwork; indeed she needed to hand in monthly reports so that her supervisors would know how the work went on, and fieldnotes made up the reports naturally. However, she soon realised that by writing for others, she tended to disguise such things as the deep frustration when she couldn't find any field site, the sense of confusion when the observations didn't support her arguments, the helplessness when the bits and pieces seemed unrelated to each other. This concealed an important part of her fieldwork – her personal journey in the field. Therefore it is better to make your own fieldnotes separated from the reports you write up for others (your fieldnotes could be the basis for reports).

Make a habit of re-reading your notes. Gradually, you will start reading them as a source of 'data' which you can group, catalogue and convert into preliminary analyses. You will also notice that the entries gradually become shorter and more focused. The entries of the first days in fieldwork might be very short as well – you feel that there is very little to report on as yet – but the opening stages of fieldwork usually result in long entries, because *everything is still new.* You find yourself in a strange environment in which you need to find your bearings; every aspect of that experience is new, strange, puzzling. The more you get used to your environment (and your environment gets used to you), the more you 'normalise' the conduct, social relations and encounters you experience. You don't see them as marked and deviant anymore, and you don't feel that they are in need of description and explanation any more: they have become *your* social and cultural codes, no longer just *theirs.* Thus, the longer you dwell in the field, the less you will report on 'strange' events and encounters and the more you will start focusing on the business at hand: talks you have with informants, bits of material you transcribed and annotated, reports of visits to libraries, documentation centres, archives, addresses and phone numbers of new contacts, *aide-mémoires* to send material to certain people upon your return, and so forth. Your fieldnotes, like the other records you keep, thus testify to the shift in your own gaze and attention as you start learning and become familiar with the environment in which you work and live.

> In Dong Jie's notebook you could find anything – from drawings of the schools to photos of pupils' performances. Figure 4.3 is a drawing

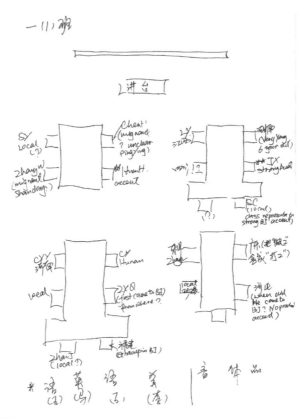

Figure 4.3 Classroom layout

of the classroom layout[6] that Dong Jie made on the very first day in the school. Although organising class around groups was perhaps only natural for the teachers and pupils, this was striking for Dong Jie – when she was in school all pupils sat in rows, and she didn't expect any difference in this sense. The fact that pupils sat around table and did group work was very telling in Dong Jie's eyes initially, but this sort of observations quickly lost the charm as Dong Jie gradually settled into school routines and became one of the community.

Less things will *amaze* or *surprise* you, and these feeling of surprise and amazement are what Agar (1995) calls **'rich points'** in ethnography: moments at which you think 'hey, that's strange' or 'what the hell is this?' (Agar provides an excellent illustration of this; see also Fabian's 1991 'Rule and Process' for similar accounts.)[7] This feeling is important: it indicates that *you bumped into the boundary of what is readily understandable for you* – the boundaries of your cultural and social conventions – and that the event that caused the surprise fell outside your established, familiar categories of understanding. Such feelings, or rich points to continue with Agar's term, are the start of ethnographic investigation: in order to make sense of what happened, you need to cross the line and try to get into the other's cultural and social world, find out the contexts for what happened and start using these instead of your own contextualisations in interpreting what goes on. The length of your fieldnotes in the initial stages of fieldwork suggests that the days were littered with 'rich points', and that you bumped into the boundaries of your own sociocultural codes on every street corner. The fact that they decrease in length and density later on shows that there are less and less 'rich points', and that you have started adopting a lot of the local codes, customs and patterns of conduct. Your fieldnotes provide an archive of that immensely important process, and it is of crucial importance that you recognise them as such: as a repository of rich points that emerge, get explained, and disappear because they are *known*.

Do not think that you need an exotic environment to experience rich points. Of course, when a sophisticated urbanite from New York, London or Berlin arrives in a native village deep in the Amazon Forest, chances are that s/he will only experience rich points, that the whole world is one big rich point. But that is just a matter of degree, not of substance. Even while doing research in an environment of which you think that it is familiar, you will be surprised and amazed – you will come across rich points. Research in one's own immediate neighbourhood usually results in an awareness of how little one actually knew about it prior to the inquiries; research in a school in which one spent years as a pupil or a teacher may likewise yield surprises.

There are two main reasons for that. First, we tend to have a unified, homogeneous image of our own life world. Everything looks simple and straightforward; the people all look the same and speak the same language. A few days of research will teach you that this erstwhile familiar environment now appears to contain at least three or four subcultures, microcosms where things are very different from what you expected and populated by people who are rather sharply different from what you thought they were. You discover that people in your neighbourhood have widely divergent interests, do their shopping in very different places, watch very different TV channels, and talk with accents you never picked up before. Societies are a patchwork of micro-units, they only *look* homogeneous. Second, as a fieldworker, you tend to start asking questions that no one normally asks; you tend to establish connections between the here-and-now and other contexts, connections that no one ever established; you tend to problematise things that nobody ever calls into question (and you problematise them perhaps precisely because of that). In other words, you have a very different orientation towards social reality, one that takes nothing for granted and which treats everything which is considered 'normal' as suspect, intriguing and worthy of some investigation.

Interviewing

We should probably begin by correcting a widespread error. Many people call their research 'ethnographic' when it contains interviews. In fact, it is very common to see 'ethnographic' and 'interview' as a fixed collocation: 'I will use *ethnographic interviews* to inquire into X'. Let it be clear right from the start: there is nothing intrinsically ethnographic about an interview, and doing interviews does not make your research ethnographic. As we discussed earlier, research is ethnographic because it accepts a number of fundamental principles and views on social reality. Consequently, interviews can be thoroughly non-ethnographic: when they are decontextualised, massacred, and reduced to something that never happened in a real interaction. A former friend of Jan's, a historian who had done extensive studies on recollections from ex-soldiers in the Nazi SS, once proclaimed that he re-used the tapes on which he recorded his interviews. He recorded them, went home, threw out all the questions from his transcript and reduced the answers of the respondents to a prose story. Afterwards the sound recording was destroyed and replaced by another one. That, ladies and gentlemen, is non-ethnographic interviewing, and the man ceased to be Jan's friend at once.

Another widespread belief which demands qualification is that interviews are the 'core' of your data, that they are *the* data you should bring back from the field. And yet another is that interviews are strange, specialised forms of interaction that require extensive preparation, training and technique. Many people think of Jeremy Paxman on BBC Newsnight when they think of interviewing.

As for the first assumption: it should be clear that you are supposed to bring back far more than just some recorded interviews. You have observed events and processes on a daily basis and these observations have found their way in hundreds of pages of fieldnotes; you have made recordings and photographs, and (as we shall see in the next section) you have collected bags full of ethnographic rubbish. Your interviews will represent but a tiny fraction of the materials you bring back and of the 'data' that will inform your work. They are important, to be sure, but they are not *more* important than the other kinds of materials. As for the second assumption: interviews usually go wrong when you conduct them like Jeremy Paxman does on Newsnight. We shall have more to say about that below.

There are some excellent books on ethnographic interviewing, and the most outstanding one is undoubtedly Charles Briggs' *Learning How To Ask* (1986, recently republished). Briggs treats fieldwork interviewing from a linguistic-anthropological perspective, as a socioculturally loaded communicative activity in its own right. He emphasises that interviews, like every form of human interaction, always have a metalevel. It is not just *what* people tell you, but also *how* they tell it that requires our attention. Someone may be very confident in giving answers, but his answer to one particular question is hesitant, pronounced somewhat softer than the others, with a body language that articulates discomfort. The respondent here communicates something *about* what he says: he signals that he feels awkward, ill at ease, uncertain, embarrassed about what he says, and that perhaps this is a topic he'd rather close than continue. Briggs draws our attention to these metapragmatic (meaning: something that comments on the action) levels of communication in fieldwork interviews; he demonstrates that overlooking them may sometimes lead you to very wrong conclusions, and he focuses our eyes on the communicative complexity and the density in meanings that characterise such encounters.

Briggs' book should be read and thoroughly read. There is no substitute for it. We will use his basic insights in what follows, and will restrict our discussion to comments on a number of points:

(1) Interviews are conversations.
(2) You are part of the interview.
(3) The importance of anecdotes.
(4) No such thing as a bad interview.

Before embarking on these comments we should remind you of the fact that many of the points raised with respect to recordings also apply to interviews. People tend to perceive them as slightly threatening, formal and abnormal speech situations (often because they expect you to start behaving like Jeremy Paxman), and they know that they 'go on record'. So there might be conditions imposed on interviewing and the use of interviews. Also, and similar to what we said above, because of this sensitivity, you should again not be cavalier about your interview sessions. Make appointments and *keep them*, prepare well and check your equipment, better a handful of good ones than a large number of insignificant ones, listen to the interview soon after the recording session, and if the situation favours it, make notes during the session. Like in every other aspect of fieldwork, this creates good conditions for successful work but does not ensure that your work is successful. Outside forces might conspire against you – as when a cleaning lady decided to start vacuum cleaning the living room, right in the middle of a long and concentrated interview by Jan with a very old informant whose voice was rather weak and unclear anyway. There is nothing one can do about that (alas!) other than to curse the gods of science and commerce.

An interview is a conversation

Never behave like an interviewer: people will behave like interviewees. They will try to keep their answers brief and to the point, formulate them in factual declarative sentences, and ask at the end 'next question?' Interviews are conversations: a particular kind of conversation, but a conversation nonetheless. It is an *ordered* conversation, one that is structured by questions or topics you may want to see discussed (more on that further on), and one in which you (the interviewer) will have to make sure that a particular order is being followed. The interview becomes something special *afterwards*, when you take its recorded version back home and start using it as 'data'.

But apart from that, the interview responds to precisely the same kinds of opportunities and constraints as 'ordinary' conversation. That means: it is dialogical in the sense that both parties contribute to it. That also means that things such as *rapport* are crucial: does the interviewee like you or not? If s/he finds you not too sympathetic (or when you find him/her not too sympathetic) chances are that there won't be much of an interview. *Cooperativity* is another factor: there must be a shared desire to talk to one another. If one of the two parties decides that this is rubbish and withdraws in deep taciturnity, or starts checking email while you try to continue the interview, or looks at his/her watch every two minutes, the result may be rather poor, and predictably so.

> In an earlier research project, Dong Jie interviewed socially disadvantaged people in London. Initially she held a list of questions and went through them with the interviewees; soon it attracted Dong Jie's attention that the interviewees only gave short and focused answers, sometimes with brief explanations if Dong Jie insisted on more details. There was not much more information yielded from the interviews than from structured questionnaires. The interviewees' dry and factual responses also influenced Dong Jie, as she struggled to get more out of

the interviews. Were socially disadvantaged people reluctant to talk about what they had in their mind? Perhaps, but many of the interviewees became very vocal and expressive as soon as Dong Jie put the list down, which meant 'the interview finished and we can chat on whatever you/we like'. It could be the list that troubled the interviewees (as well as the interviewer) – they thought about the next question while answering the current one. Answering against a list also made them feel that they were questioned by rather than talked to Dong Jie, which made the interactions awkward. The interviewees appeared more relaxed and talkative without a list, and Dong Jie rarely forgot any topic she wanted to talk about.

Things such as *formality/informality* and *politeness* also play a role. Like in every human interaction there are rules to be observed: rules of distance, of not transgressing certain boundaries (e.g. the use of rude language or insults, sexual or racial abuse and misconduct, rules of social status recognition, etc.). And if your interlocutor sees you as someone who takes undue liberties with him/her, a swift end to the interview (as well as a very bad reputation for the interviewer afterwards) is to be expected. And finally, like every human interaction interviews are also prone to *misunderstanding*: 'technical' misunderstanding as when a name of word is not correctly understood, 'pragmatic' misunderstanding as when, for example, a joke is misunderstood as a serious statement (or vice versa), or 'cognitive' misunderstanding as when someone produces a statement you simply cannot comprehend. Our social world is unfortunately sprinkled with misunderstandings between human beings, so why should an interview be any different?[8]

Do not expect your interviews to be perfect instances of communication in which both speakers manage to talk in absolute clarity and faultless sentences, producing relevant new information in every sentence. Interviews are like everyday conversations: messy, complex, often containing contradictions and statements that are made off the top of one's head, with people shifting topics and getting lost in details, losing the line of their argument, not finding the exact words for what they wish to say, and with *silences*, hesitations, pauses. Recording devices often have a 'voice activation' tool; if you switch it on it will only record when there is an audible voice. Never ever switch that thing on. If you do, you would lose that crucial part of conversations which we call silence. Silences are not an absence of speech, they are the production of silence, they are very much part of speech. We produce silence when we need to think, when we hesitate (i.e. when we find something sensitive, controversial or emotional), when we do not wish to say something.

The interviewer must be silent at times: it is a prerequisite for the other to talk. If the interviewee can't get a word in edgewise, the interview may not be as rich as you expected it to be. Your silence, in addition, can be a powerful instrument of elicitation. If you ask a question and the interviewee gives an answer, s/he will expect you to take over straight away after the conclusion of the answer. If you remain silent for a moment and continue to hold your 'listening' body posture, the interviewee will continue to talk, for s/he will think that you're not satisfied with the answer, or that you believe the answer is incomplete (raising your eyebrows when you sit there silent may be a particularly powerful prompt, but it often triggers an embarrassed reaction from the interviewee). It is a natural feature of conversational structure in many cultures that long silences are to be avoided, and if the other one doesn't speak, you will. Be aware of this dynamic: it will make your interviewees be more generous and talkative. They will break into anecdotes, repeat what they said with more details, and so on.

> This was a useful tactic in Dong Jie's research, although it was not very easy to use in the beginning, because in Dong Jie's culture the one who initiates a conversation (such as the one who asks for a talk, who invites the other one, and here the one who interviews) has more responsibility than the other one to keep a conversation going, otherwise people would regard him or her as being shy or asocial. It's worth trying this tactic, however, and Dong Jie found it was not as uncomfortable as she thought.

But the interviewer should not be the silent one. It is a conversation, so conversational engagement is expected of you, and it should be 'natural' conversational engagement, not something like 'all right, thank you; the next question is . . .' or 'could you please stay to the point'. You must provide the natural reactions and responses of surprise, amazement, interest, fascination, amusement that someone expects in a conversation: the nodding, the 'uh uh', 'mhh', 'yes', 'really?' must all be there, along with a sufficient dose of 'that's interesting'. If someone engages in a story, do not try to cut him/her off (we shall see below why this is relevant). Provide reactions with a rising intonation ('yes?') and you will get more. In general, try to be a good, interested and sympathetic listener, who every now and then provides some stories and recollections of his/her own. Do provide such supporting narratives, they can be very helpful in getting more and more detailed information.

A conversation is *not an interrogation*. It is talk between people on a variety of topics. We emphasise *topics*, not *questions*, because (as Hymes said in the beginning of this book) not all there is to be found out can be found out by *asking*. Not everyone has an opinion about everything, and sometimes, your question could be the first time they are asked to *form* an opinion about it. It is better therefore to develop *topics*. Rather than introducing something as a question, you introduce it as something you'd like to talk about 'I'm interested in ... and I've seen that you ...'. The topic, then, will be gradually developed – your statement won't have the bombshell effect of a point-blank question – and people can qualify what they have to say ('I don't know much about it, but ...'), make comments about *how* they know something ('I've been there quite often and ...', 'I've only heard it from others') and offer what they have to offer.[9] By carefully developing the topic you'll discover how the interviewee relates to what s/he says: s/he can only talk about it in anecdotes, or is able to provide general statements interspersed with examples; s/he heavily relies on 'borrowed discourses' (e.g. phrases handed down from the media or from public fora) or talks in very much his/her own words, is sure about what s/he says or displays lots of doubts and hesitations and so on. By offering your own bits, you can find out whether s/he knows about them ('I recently saw a report on TV in which ...' – 'Oh yes, I saw it too!') or not, whether your information comes as a surprise or fits into his/her view of things and so on. All of that information is crucial, and it is easier to release when one is involved in an 'ordinary' conversation than in a question-and-answer sequence where one very often feels put on the spot by direct questions.

As to *topics*, here too you must realise that an interview is just a conversation. Not every topic can be broached in any conversation, and some topics will be seen as sensitive by some people and not by others. For some topics, you need particular context conditions (e.g. a life history usually requires a long interview, it cannot be done in half an hour), and so on. So too in interviews. Not all of your informants will volunteer their opinion on any topic (if they have an opinion on it!), some topics cannot be launched abruptly but need some preparatory lines of discussion, some topics can simply not be opened because you know the answer beforehand: denial, rejection, closure of the conversation. A few examples: very few people self-qualify as 'racists', and very few men would happily go on record that they believe that men are superior to women. Few people indeed would qualify themselves as 'radical' or 'fundamentalist', few would openly admit that they would favour a dictatorship over a democratic system, few would commit themselves publicly to eugenetic views and so on. So if you open an interview by asking 'are you a racist?', the answer would be very predictable: 'No. Next question'.

The tactic you use to discuss such sensitive topics is by taking an ***indirect*** route. Rather than 'racism' and 'racist', you use more circumspect descriptions – things that circulate publicly as *euphemisms* on racism. So you don't use the loaded words themselves, but you carefully work your way through a series of issues *that together belong to and make up the field of racism*. You could talk about the quality of schools where there are large numbers of immigrant children (a typical 'objectification' of racism is that one doesn't send one's kids to a 'coloured' school because 'the level of academic achievement in such schools is low' and 'one wants only the best for the kids'); or about safety problems in the inner cities (where you could bump into another widespread image: the direct correlation between crime and the presence of immigrants); or about issues of security (where you are likely to meet the collocation of *Muslim* terrorism), and so on. People can talk in a very reasonable and moderate way for hours, constructing a tower of meanings which taken together is very irrational and radical.[10] Please note, and this is very important, that *you can do an interview on racism without mentioning the term or without announcing your interview as being on racism*. This is not a violation of any ethical rule, you are not lying to your informants or misguiding them, and there are two reasons for that: (1) You don't have to *mention* racism to *talk about* racism; most of us have experiences in which we talked about something while pretending to talk about something else; (2) 'racism' in your research is an *analytical category*, not a term. You have constructed your own 'field' of racism in preparing the ground: various kinds of related activities, ideas and images have been grouped under that term. The word 'racism', therefore, has a deeply different scope and meaning that it has in the everyday respondent's mind. You are looking for one 'racism', your informants may have quite another one in mind. Using the term, on the assumption that the word would be crystal clear and perfectly similar in meaning for you and for your informant, would be ludicrous.[11]

> In Dong Jie's fieldwork of rural migrant pupils in urban schools, the word 'discrimination' was very sensitive, in a society of largely egalitarian ideology. It would be very offensive if Dong Jie asked directly 'are the rural pupils discriminated', or 'are local children more important than migrant pupils'. Even migrant pupils and their parents rarely acknowledged the unequal status they had compared to those of local pupils. However, talking about who should be student leaders or win merit student awards, the teachers were surprisingly straightforward: definitely local pupils, because outstanding records would be helpful for them to continue to secondary school – those who held such awards would have a better chance of getting into the good secondary schools. What about migrant pupils? They usually had to either go back to their

hometown/village for secondary education or to an appointed school which was normally one of the underachieving secondary schools in the district, and therefore titles and awards to them would be wasted. The teachers were frank about this because it was not a case of discrimination as far as they were concerned, but thinking practically.

You are part of the interview

It is very clear by now: the 'interview' is not just the part in which your respondent speaks; it is very much a dialogue with you, and you also build, construct and make the interview into what it is. This is important, because as mentioned earlier, it is a widespread practice in a lot of research to erase the interviewer's questions and interventions from the record of the interview. It is as if the interviewer wasn't there or had no other effect than to push buttons that set the respondent talking – the interviewer as the neutral extension of the tape recorder. And so an 'interview' is usually understood to be 'what the interviewee said'. That the interviewer had a tremendous influence on what was said and how it was said (in other words: that nothing that the interviewee said could come about *without* the interviewer's active input) escapes the attention of the researchers.

Let us not commit that error. As an interviewer engaged in an ordered conversation with the interviewee, your impact is enormous, and *this impact is part of your 'data'*. When a respondent voices radical opinions, they should be contextualised: it could be an effect of the way in which you framed and pitched the issue; had you used other formulations the opinions may have come across as less radical. You co-construct the interview, and every statement made by the interviewee is a statement that reflects your presence and your level and mode of participation.

That means that *your turns in the interview also need to be transcribed and analysed*. An analysis of the interview is never just an analysis of what the interviewee said, it is an *analysis of a dialogue between you and the interviewee*. Usually that is a source of deep embarrassment. In re-listening to the interview, you will have to spend an equal amount of attention to your own voice and statements as to those of the interviewee. And for most of us, that means a painful confrontation with badly formulated statements, errors in comprehension, missed opportunities in the interview, your own accent, your irritating insistence on particular points and so on. It is not a nice, but often an illuminating experience, and it makes you into a better interviewer: you will discover, analytically, what you do in such dialogues, and in so doing you will learn from your mistakes.

In a recorded interview fragment two young interviewees were telling Dong Jie the rarely spoken issue of discrimination – the girl said something like the local pupils looked down on them (migrant children). She then gave as an example that the student leaders (all of whom were local pupils) often picked on migrant pupils and blamed them for any mistake. Dong Jie was perhaps too excited by the unexpected story the pupil told her – instead of letting her tell more of that story, Dong Jie unfortunately turned to the other pupil and asked whether he had similar experiences. Unfortunately, the boy did not have much to say about that and soon changed the topic. Dong Jie tried a few times to bring the conversation back on track but the break finished and the pupils had to go back to their chairs. It was a pity, and there is nothing we can do but to learn from mistakes.

Your involvement in the interview also has wider dimensions. As an interviewer, you will often be imagined as a figure of *authority*. You approach people with the label of researcher stuck on you, someone affiliated with the prestige institution we call the university, and surrounded by assumptions of intellectual brilliance and sophistication. In addition to that, most of us are clearly and identifiably middle class people, we carry some expensive equipment and so on. We are a particular kind of people, and this usually differs from our informants; they consequently have a particular set of images about us and a set of expectations about us. Nobody enters an interview situation as a blank page; as soon as you enter, you are someone.

Let us look at an example of how the interviewer influences the interviewee. The example below is a small fragment of an interview in which two young female Belgian researchers (both in their early 20s) talk with a 16-year-old female high school student from a poor township near Cape Town, South Africa. The interviewers are identified by M and N in the transcript; the interviewee by E. The interviewee is from Xhosa descent, which means that according to South African criteria she is 'black'; English is the language of instruction in school and is not her native language. The two interviewers are obviously 'white', and for them as well English is not their native language. We will emphasise some features of the transcript in **bold** and *bold italics*.

1	**M:**	ehr do you . like ehr . going to school?
2	**E:**	**[quietly] yah xxxxx**
3	**M:**	this one *you like /
4	**N:**	yeah?
5	**E:**	yes it's very nice /
6	**M:**	how come? … why do you like it / or

7	**E:**	ehr it's the first / it is the first time tha' we have a *community school here in westbank/ and now come together to school so
8	**M:**	yeah
9	**E:**	.. like .. meeting new people .. and sort of . we are getting *proud* of our school
10	**M:**	You're *pride* of your school?
11	**E:**	yeah we *pride*
12	**N:**	do you like all the courses . that you follow here?
13	**E:**	**yes miss**

The point here is to see how the interviewers are given a particular identity of authority here by the interviewee. In line 2, we see that the first question by M is answered by a quiet and almost inaudible answer from E (the xxxx signals something which could not be understood from the recording, so it was spoken very quietly). Naturally, this pitch level signals that E is not very much at ease. This is a strange format for her: two 'white' women talking to her. Being 'white' is still something very different from being 'black' in South Africa: it immediately projects identities of superiority and power; E seems to absorb these. She is also not very familiar with the question-and-answer format of the interview, and we see how she searches for a frame in which she can organise her own behaviour. The frame she finds is that of classroom Q-and-A; we see this in line 13, when she calls N 'miss' – the label she normally uses for her schoolteacher. The 'yes miss' is a classroom response.

But there is more. In lines 9–11, the interviewee adopts an error introduced by the interviewer. In line 9, she says correctly 'we are getting proud of our school'. This is followed up by M as 'you're pride of your school' – in which we see 'proud' being replaced by 'pride', incorrectly. The girl adopts 'we pride' in line 11, rather than 'proud' as in line 9. What we see here is that the interviewer, clearly, is also a figure of authority *in English*. An incorrect expression by the interviewer is ratified (positively sanctioned by repeating it) by the interviewer. The interviewer here not only shapes the particular information produced in the interview, but also the particular linguistic ways in which this information is communicated to her. In this particular case – a South African township school – historical relations of superiority and inferiority (articulated in 'race': white versus black) creep into the interview and give it an importance beyond the immediate event. What we see here is how the interviewer–interviewee relation becomes an instance of old, deeply entrenched group relations in the country. A white person is almost by definition 'right', a black one 'wrong'.

It is very, very hard to manoeuvre such factors, as they belong to the living reality in which fieldwork takes place. You cannot become 'black' if you are 'white', a woman when you are a man, young when you are old and vice versa. You can *act* young when you're old, or pretend to be working class if you are upper class, but there will be moments where that role cannot be sustained, where age and class features suddenly occur and start twisting the event in peculiar directions. You cannot be someone or something else in fieldwork, and it is wise not to try too hard being someone or something else: you cannot keep it up. You are not an extension of your tape recorder: you're not a nicely manufactured Sony XC350, but you are Marianne Jones or Josh Patel, PhD researcher at the Institute of Education, someone who is a real person in interaction with someone else, who also is not just 'data', but a real person.

The importance of anecdotes

If your interviews are conceived of and conducted as conversations, they will contain the features of ordinary conversations, and one of the well-known features of that is *narrative*. Whenever we talk, we construct our talk around stories, big and small. We call such stories 'anecdotes', and this suggests that they are not very important, just scaffolding for an argument, illustrations or embellishment (or boring!). In fact, anecdotes are the raw diamonds in fieldwork interviews. They are often your best and most valued 'facts'.

The reason is that in narratives, people produce very complex sociocultural meanings. It is through an anecdote that we see what exactly they understand by a particular term, how our questions resonate in their own life worlds, how relevant it is, how their own life worlds are structured, which influences they articulate. We also see, by attending to anecdotes, that they have *cognitive, affective (emotional) and argumentative* functions. Telling an anecdote not only provides knowledge and organises it in a particular way. It also provides hints at how the storyteller relates to that knowledge (whether she likes it or not, whether she is confident about it or not, whether it is a thing that upsets her or leaves her unaffected …). And it also shows us how particular bits of experience and knowledge are invoked to support, modify or attack an argument. Anecdotes, in sum, contain all the stuff we are after.

Consider the following example. It is a translated part of a Dutch interview between two students (T and B) and a male asylum seeker from Ivory Coast (R). The fragment is from the beginning of the interview, and it is an answer to the question: 'why did you leave the Ivory Coast?'

R: (sighs) **yeah/for *everyone it is difficult to understand the politics of the Ivory Coast because/ it is never discussed**/ but over there

we still have the *French army/ ehr ehr our airport is a French army
base/ and these people are there anyway and we=we=we have no
right to choose our=our own government/ yes these people are
appointed by France/ but we are *not a colony anymore...since
thirty-eight years we ehr have obtained our independence/ but until
now our ministers have always been appointed by France...our
country is in the center of West-Africa/ and that is a strategic
position

T: =yes yes

R: yes/so...yes there is=we are not rich/ and..okay..eight years ago we
tried to create political par–parties and so [louder] but the government
itself has created *thirty-eight parties/ while this is the difficult thing
to ehr get elected or to lead a country.. If you are not a member of a
party/ *then they=we obtained different ehr permission to create
parties/ and apart from that or on *top of that the government has
created thirty eight parties/ apart from the=*plus the thehh
monopartism like that

T: yes

R: yes the monopartism exists since sixty/ till ninety/ thirty years/ and
yes they have themselves created thirty=thirty-eight parties/ the
people who *don=t work for the government/ I mean/ in ehr..the=the
private the private sector is very small/ everyone already works
for=for the government/ and if.. yes the people who work for the
government they are like ehr the prison/ they are like imprisoned/
because you..you=you are always afraid of losing your job/ maybe in
your family with your nephews and nieces and so maybe you are
about one hundred people and you are the only one who has a job/
that/ yes/ all these other people are/ they=they are poor and they all
count on you / then you have to keep your job *if not *someone from
your family will be bought to be used against you/ yes things like
that..small things like that/ and we...yes [sighs] yes there is our
president of our party [points to a picture on the wall] / we also
have=we also try to get organised here in Belgium in Holland in
France/ the=the large group is in France in Italy in Germany also in
other countries..in Holland/ the people from Holland will come here
the day after tomorrow we have our/ yes large meeting in Brussels...
that=s it...yes thehh reason was that in nine=ninety five/ we had to
do an election/ and in thirty four=ninety four a list of all the
*inhabitants had to be made/ but the people who did that when they
came to you and they know that you are a=a member of the
opposition/ then your name=ehr your name would not be written
down/ and if your name is not written down you can=t vote/ and

that=s what they did/ yes we tried to find that list/ yes and make
another one

B: yes

R: but that was illegal

B: yes

R: if it/ yes/ then we are prosecuted/ **and so I had to escape/**

The answer to the question is, as we see, not a straightforward and
linear one, beginning with 'because'. The answer in that narrow sense is
given at the end of the fragment: 'and so I had to escape'. What precedes
is a long and complex narrative which displays a lot of structure and offers
lots and lots of information. Let us look at the way in which this story is
constructed by R.

Why did you escape from the Ivory Coast?

Point of departure

1. For everyone it is difficult to understand the politics of the Ivory Coast

General reason: neocolonialism

2. We still have the French army
3. And we have no right to choose our own government
        {reasons:} we are in the centre of West-Africa
4.   {that is why the French are there, because} we are not rich

Specific reason: membership of political opposition party

5. Eight years ago we tried to create political parties
6.   {this is problematical, because} the government itself has created
          38 parties
          {the government manipulates the democratization process:
          monopartyism plus 38 bogus parties}
          {iron grip of the régime on society} you are always afraid of losing
          your job
7.   {our party also exists in Europe}
8. The *{immediate} reason* was {election fraud}
          {the régime tried to commit fraud in voter registration}
          {we tried to counterfeit our own voter registration list}
          but that was illegal

Conclusion

9. Then we are prosecuted and so I had to escape

We see that R starts his story with what we can call an epistemic
framing: 'For everyone it is difficult to understand the politics of the

Ivory Coast'. This means: I'll have to tell you something in order for you to understand my reasons, and I will have to tell you something not just about myself but about politics in the Ivory Coast. This, clearly, is a reflection of experience. Like so many asylum seekers, R had had the experience of having to tell his story of escape over and over again to authorities and support agencies, and of being either not heard or not understood by them. So we now know that the story he tells us is an *important* story for him, a story which he considers crucial for us to understand why he has applied for asylum.

The story itself, then, starts from a broad perspective: that of neo-colonialism. This, of course, has at first sight very little worth as an answer to the question as to why *he* fled his country. But its function becomes clear afterwards. He moves from neo-colonialism to the problems facing new opposition parties in his country, and to his own involvement in one such movement, and his part in events surrounding the elections. Note that he ends his story with 'but that was illegal'. R had indeed broken the law in his country, and this proved to be disastrous for his asylum application, since people who have committed criminal acts cannot get asylum. The whole contextual story, starting with neo-colonialism and ending with his involvement in election fraud, is meant to offer arguments for seeing his illegal behaviour as legitimate: not his actions were illegitimate, but the laws he broke are neo-colonial laws that need to be broken in order to create a democracy in his country.

Many a researcher would dismiss this long and winding story as irrelevant or as 'babble', providing hardly any hard facts. In effect, the way in which such stories are received by asylum authorities is to scrap all such anecdotes and reduce the story to a sequence of established facts. Yet, the narrative provides crucial clues to understanding such 'facts': R here provides all kinds of connections between his own personal predicament and larger factors influencing it; he articulates his own political, social and moral position while doing so; and he tells us something about his experiences with intercultural communication in Belgium by saying that 'For everyone it is difficult to understand the politics of the Ivory Coast': Belgians usually don't know anything about this, and if they do they don't listen or don't care about it.

Thus, in your interviews, try to have people produce stories, anecdotes. If they embark on one, let them do so and do not interrupt it, even if some voice in your head tells you that the informant is getting side-tracked. S/he is only getting sidetracked in *your* universe, in relation to your research questions. But *the side-tracking may be precisely what there is to find out*: a connection between things, one that you had not previously spotted, but which the informant establishes by his/her seemingly erratic and weird jump from one topic to another. Things that in your world are disconnected may be solidly connected in their life worlds, and anecdotes offer you a rich way into that. The story provides you with contexts, experiences, motives, fragments of what Bourdieu called 'practical reason': the way in which people build argumentative constructs out of their socially and culturally conditioned experiences, and how such arguments help them to make sense of their world.

No such thing as a bad interview

This leads us to another issue. What is a *good* interview and what is a *bad* interview? When does an interview yield the 'data' you're after? The answer to that is by no means simple, as each time there will be real yardsticks and objectives, specific to the piece of research you intend to do. But the rule of thumb is: every interview yields *something*, and often it yields something in unexpected ways.

The reason for that is that every interview *produces* something: a discourse organised between two parties (interviewer and interviewee) in a particular context. Such discourses may be rich and dense (ideal data! Best examples!) but they can also be shallow and thin. The interviewee is less than forthcoming, withdrawn and shy; reluctant and resistant to your introducing particular topics or arguments. S/he looks down on you and imposes a line of answering that does not satisfy your expectations. S/he restricts him/herself to the production of commonplaces and hand-me-downs from media discourses or institutional ones.

The example given earlier, of the township high school student, could be read as such a failure. It was clear that the girl assumed a very submissive stance towards the interviewers, and even that she produced echoes of the interviewers' voices in her responses. This could be a failure if we see this from an angle in which we are out to find 'pure', uncontaminated evidence – these data are obviously contaminated by the interviewer. Similarly, the long narrative produced by the man from Ivory Coast could also be seen as a 'bad' case, because he takes us on an endless tour of the history of West Africa, distorting a swift flux of well-targeted information. Both can be turned into *successful* pieces of work, though, as we have seen. In both instances, looking carefully into the issue of positioning – your own and that of the informant – reveals that our informants there were following a particular logic, a contextual logic which reveals how they see us, the information we are asking for, and themselves. Thus, interviews that fail to produce one kind of data can still yield another kind of data: data about the context, about social positions from which people speak. And such positions generate and constrain the discourses they can produce.

> One of Dong Jie's main respondents was the teacher of the class that Dong Jie observed for several months. She and Dong Jie spent a lot of time together exchanging ideas about the pupils, and she saw Dong Jie as an educational researcher (i.e. expert) who would be able to help her with problems she came across in practice. The teacher's main concerns were about two underachieving pupils; to Dong Jie's disappointment, both pupils were local, while Dong Jie's research interest was in migrant pupils. The teacher talked about the two pupils for hours, how hard it was to help them, what influence they had from their families, etc., but Dong Jie desperately wanted to set their conversations on the track of migrant pupils. At the end Dong Jie saw the day wasted although she was loaded with fieldnotes on and recorded interviews of the two local pupils. Reluctantly, she did her routine job and went through the data she'd got during the day (reading fieldnotes and listening to the recordings) ... but hang on, what was she saying here 'they are even not as good as XXX (a migrant pupil who was also considered underachieving), and there 'they are not popular among other local pupils, but they do make friends with XXX and XXX (both were migrant pupils)'. Why the teacher was concerned with the local pupils, not the migrant ones, although all of them had unsatisfactory results? Did the two pupils feel excluded by their local peers? Did they prefer to make friends with migrant children given their different backgrounds? The conversations turned out to produce interesting staring points for further inquiries.

Imagine that the topic of your work is unemployment, and that among your respondents you have a number of unemployed people and a number of employers. Obviously and predictably, they will produce very different answers to the same questions. None of the answers is intrinsically 'better' than the other; both answers reveal the particular position from which they see this bit of reality. And what they say (and how they say it) will reveal traces of their positions. It is not unlikely that the interview with the unemployed respondent will be emotionally charged, full of anger and frustration, strongly connected to his/her own life world and everyday experiences, and with very little references to macro-economic issues. It is also not unlikely that the discourse of the employer would be more detached, more factual and unemotional, and that there would be abundant references to the larger economic and political dimensions of the issue. These data are incomparable and incompatible: it makes very little sense to try and 'measure' who speaks the truth and provides the best diagnosis of the problem. Both, however, reflect different positions from which they see the problem, and in that sense lead you into the way in which social structure influences the way we see the world. These are great data.

Thus, when people are taciturn in an interview, their taciturnity becomes data and needs to be examined. Is it because the respondent does not know anything about this? Or feels that s/he has nothing significant to say about it? Or that the topic invokes painful personal experiences that cannot be communicated in this manner? Or that s/he feels that this is so delicate a topic that s/he wants to be prudent when going on record? Or that your recording device scares him/her? Or that s/he feels that you are not in a position to ask such questions (who do you think you are!), or that the way you put them testifies to a lack of tact and politeness? Or that you are intimidating to him/her? All of this is possible, and interesting to look into, because again the answer to such questions can bring you closer to understanding a fundamental point: that not everyone in a society has access to the same discourses, and that certain discourses can only be produced under certain circumstances.[12] Don't be discouraged when an interview of which you expected a lot is finished after 20 minutes of superficial talk. Ask why it went that way, and think about the different contextual possibilities for that event. A failure will quickly become a success.

Collecting Rubbish

Ethnographers are notorious for collecting rubbish. In their anxiety not to overlook a single piece of information that might be the key stone to their interpretation, they collect everything: objects, texts, newspaper clippings, audio and video tapes, books and booklets, flyers, announcements, advertisements … name it, you will find it in the ethnographer's bags upon return to the home or academic base camp. All of this is collected in an attempt to get as rich a picture as possible of the environment in which the fieldwork was done. It combines with photographs, recordings and fieldnotes into one huge pile of materials that, together, allow us to make a careful reconstruction of the place, time and occasion on which we did our work. It helps us remember and recall features, details, characters, an atmosphere we found crucial for our understanding of what went on. And since we are always distrustful of our own memory, we collect it, catalogue it, describe it, and carry it with us back home.

We are saying this to the chagrin of mothers, partners and roommates and we shall be cursed by them: *do collect that kind of rubbish*. It is very much similar to making photographs, recordings and fieldnotes: they are essential ingredients of your record, of the archive of your own journey into knowledge. And they respond to the same laws: you will collect more rubbish in the beginning than at the end of your fieldwork, because again, you will know more about the place and less will be new and amazing. So do collect, and collect well.

There is only one rule of thumb here: like with fieldnotes, take everything that closely or remotely looks of interest. Don't be too restrictive, and even if it doesn't tell you much on the spot, it can always become a very relevant bit of data later on. There are a good number of cases in which what looked like a side issue on the spot gains prominence a lot later. It can even become a new project, or ideal data for an article. We are speaking from experience here. When Jan was in Tanzania in 1985, the topic of his fieldwork was local and national political discourse. He quickly noticed, however, that the people he spoke with produced a lot of code-switching between Swahili and English. He got intrigued by it, finding himself sometimes in the awkward position of the only speaker of 'pure' Swahili and English (and eventually being forced to learn how to do that kind of code-switching). Thus, while Jan was collecting material on his 'real' topic, another topic developed alongside it through recordings and rubbish – tapes with urban pop music in which such switching was present; letters, newspaper clippings, cartoons and so on. And by the time Jan submitted his dissertation on Swahili political style he had several published articles on code-switching in Tanzania. In spite of his best efforts, interest in that topic has never left him.

Make a point of collecting with some discipline. Use your fieldnotes to catalogue them, offer small bits of description in your notes, documenting what this particular bit of rubbish suggests or tells you about the things you're interested in. Perhaps also indicate how it could be used later in your analysis: you'll forget what it meant later in your fieldwork or after your return, and things that looked like valuable information then can quickly become just scraps of paper later.

Conclusion

Your bag is full now, and what do we have? We have background information collected during the preparation of your fieldwork; we have observations that found their way in your fieldnotes, recordings and visual materials, and we have recorded interviews. We are ready to go home now and start working on our analysis and on the daunting task of writing all of this up in a dissertation or publication.

Note that what we have in our bag is a widely divergent collection of materials. *Ethnographic fieldwork data are not uniform* but widely diverse, ranging from material artefacts over subjective notes to recordings and interviews and photographs. Together they create an archive of your own learning process. They tell a story of 'the field', to be sure, but even more eloquently they tell a story about yourself in the field, of how you became someone who started understanding things in a strange environment, thus gradually reducing the strangeness of that environment to such a point where it became a familiar place. This, then, will have to be carried over into your analysis.

Notes

1. Migrant schools in Beijing are private schools specifically for children whose parents relocate to Beijing as low-paid workers from mainly rural areas within the country; migrant schools often operate with a low budget and offer basic education.
2. Or when the wire of the microphone runs down the body and stops at the underbelly – causing giggles and suggestive winks from the pupils.
3. We disagree with a number of esteemed colleagues and ethics committees on this and invite students to seek a second opinion on this point. Sometimes the conditions imposed on recording and the use of recorded materials are absurd, curtailing the essence of research: the freedom to return to earlier work and revisit it in light of new developments or evidence. Such multiple and repeated use of existing data is essential if we want to prevent research from becoming an atomised enterprise, consisting of a myriad of unique but unconnected (and unconnectable), isolated pieces of work. We are familiar with the ethical issues involved in this and they need to be taken very seriously; but we have successfully negotiated the freedom to use recorded data beyond the particular project on a large number of occasions, often against all odds with very stubborn interlocutors. Our experience is that people, even if they are initially apprehensive, quickly grasp the importance of the argument for free use of data for research purposes.
4. In these days of micro-electronic sophistication, this is significantly easier than in the days when the fieldworker could be spotted from miles away because of the bulky tape recorder dangling from his/her shoulder. There are excellent digital audiorecorders, the size of a cigarette pack, that capture many hours of high-quality sound, can be simply uploaded on any PC through a USB connection, and come with software packages that allow editing and sound quality improvement. Even certain types of mp3 players allow such facilities. They are cheaper than any conventional device and are the best audiorecorders yet made. It is always advisable to have *more than one* recording device, again a thing which is now more affordable than a generation ago.

5. Allow us to indulge for a minute in this hopelessly romantic imagery: Jan's own field notebooks are real books, thick linen-bound notebooks filled to the brim with entries and drawings of things he saw, photos and letters stuck to the pages. Jan still uses handwriting for such purposes, and finds it important to continue doing so. Handwriting has a particular slowness and circumspect quality to it that he cannot associate with working on a PC. A PC could be stolen, while no one has ever expressed an interest in these grotesque notebooks. And the paper notebooks allowed him to write my entries late at night on a tropical beach, something which a PC would not allow. Students, by all means seek a second opinion on the topic of hand- versus computer-written fieldnotes; we are not unbiased.

6. The thin and long rectangle was a blackboard, after that was a platform for teachers. The rectangles and the 'T' shapes were tables and pupils were resembled with the small rectangles around the tables. Dong Jie tried to note down the pupils' names so that she could talk to and make friends with them soon. Besides each name was key information that Dong Jie collected on the first day about the pupils. At the bottom of the page were the class sessions for that day: morning – Chinese, English, Chinese (which should have been math, but the math teacher was sick), drawing; afternoon – music, physical exercises, humanity.

7. Fabian's well-known *Power and Performance* (1990) is completely built around such a 'rich point'. During a dinner with friends in Congo, he was offered a piece of meat; when he suggested that it should be shared with others, the answer was 'power is eaten whole'. Fabian sensed that this was a kind of proverb – here is the rich point – and started inquiring into its meaning. The explanation of this saying took months, as the friends – members of a theatre troupe – decided that the best way of demonstrating its meaning would be through the creation of a play. The play was developed, performed, and even made it to national TV in Congo.

8. Maryns (2006), in her study on asylum interviews in Belgium, provides a telling example. An African applicant tells the story of her escape. One phrase from her story was 'A man carry me to the boat'. The phrase was spoken in broken English, with a strong African accent, and the interviewers' notes and official report afterwards read: 'A man called Karimi took me to the boat'. When the applicant was afterwards questioned about the identity of this man called Karimi, she was of course extremely puzzled.

9. An interesting phenomenon, and very widespread, is that people often refer to someone else as an authority: 'you should talk to X' or 'I'm not very familiar with it, my wife knows that better'. Such statements point towards *networks* of knowledge: the ways in which people rely on others as authoritative sources on particular topics and the way in which they themselves are part of patterns of circulation of information.

10. Blommaert and Verschueren (1998) offer a detailed analysis of different 'acceptably' racist discourses.

11. Which is incidentally one of the headaches for questionnaire research: the assumption that the terms used in the questionnaire mean the same things to everyone.

12. This is one of the main themes in Blommaert (2005b): the fact that access to certain discourses is seriously constrained by all kinds of social and cultural

factors, often invisible a priori and only detectable, precisely, through 'bad' fieldwork experiences. When people don't talk, it is not always because they have no words for it, but also because they have never had an occasion to talk about it.

Read up on it

Briggs, C. (1986) *Learning How to Ask*. Cambridge: Cambridge University Press.
Sanjek, R. (ed.) (1990) *Fieldnotes: The Makings of Anthropology*. Ithaca: Cornell University Press.
Werner, O. and Schoepfle, M. (1987a) *Systematic Fieldwork Volume 1: Foundations of Ethnography and Interviewing*. Newbury Park: Sage.

Chapter 5
The Sequence 3: After Fieldwork

You are back, and after the rituals of meeting and reconnecting with family and friends,[1] you now have to start making sense of the fieldwork data. The learning process has not stopped after your return. You have started forgetting certain things, while others have assumed a clear form now. It is time for analysis and write-up.

Like in the previous chapters, we will not follow the whole potential sequence but focus on some aspects of the process that are often not addressed. Let's talk about your data and how to treat them, about the use of various data in an ethnographic argument, and about analysing narratives (your 'ideal' data). While until now we have mainly considered elements from Dong Jie's fieldwork experience, we will now also explore some of Jan's data, drawn mainly from interviews with African asylum seekers in Belgium.

Your Data

For the rest of your life, you will be referring to your 'fieldwork data'.[2] The word 'data' captures the success and achievement of fieldwork: you came back with something – something that could then be converted into scientific products and that could be used as examples, illustrations, support for arguments, in scientific discourse ('I did not find that in my data ...', 'My data tell another story ...', 'I'd like to see the data he has for that claim ...'). The word 'data' becomes emblematic of your position as a researcher. So what does it stand for?

Your data are *a complex of widely divergent scientific objects*. Together they offer *a subjective representation of facts and events 'out there', and the analysis of such data is an interpretive analysis that necessarily draws on an interdisciplinary set of methods*. Since the analysis of such data is interpretive, the boundary between 'during' and 'after' fieldwork is blurred: a lot of interpretation (read: analysis) has already been done in the field, on an everyday basis, while you were trying to make sense of the data. Your fieldnotes, thus, will already contain many pieces of analysis that will prove to be hard to improve afterwards. Let us begin with the different objects that together form your 'data'.

A kaleidoscope

You will have difficulties describing *everything* you have collected. Some things are clear: texts, material artefacts, photographs, recordings, transcripts of interviews. Most people would instantly and intuitively recognise these objects as scientific evidence for which particular procedures directed the process of collection. But your fieldnotes, for instance, are quite a bit harder to describe as scientific evidence. They contain items that are deeply personal, show no trace of 'hard facts' or of rigorous scientific procedures – they are very much a diary, and you will feel the same reticence in having other people read them as the one you had when you kept your teenage diaries. It's a very private document, yet it contains lots of invaluable information, crucial for achieving your scientific goals. And then there are things that can only be described as 'thoughts' or 'insights': immaterial things, things you just *know* because you have done your fieldwork. Features of people's character, for instance, can be essential in interpreting particular events and incidents; but of course the image you formed of people is a dialogical thing, informed by your own attitudes and preferences. Still, all of these are 'data'.

So: the fieldwork process was messy and chaotic, and this is reflected in your data. Reality is chaotic and complex, and this, too, is reflected in your data. Your data reflect the different viewpoints from which social events can be (and are) viewed: they reflect positions in relation to topics, events, phenomena. Compare it to the following image. Put a can of coca-cola on a table and walk around the table; stop at each corner of the table and describe the can from that angle. Each time you will describe the same can – the can hasn't been changed by your walk around it. But each time you will see a different side of the can and your description will be different. The 'complete' description of the can is the combination of the four descriptions you gave from four different angles. A description from any one of these angles would be a description of the can, to be sure, but it would be a partial – biased – description which represents only one viewpoint on the can.

If your fieldwork was rich and dense, your collection of data will offer you a walk around the table, so to speak. It will contain materials that reflect very different ways of addressing the same social events.

Dong Jie's fieldwork was in schools, which were hugely complex places, and her data are a collection of photos about the schools and student activities; memos from school meetings that reflect institutional viewpoints; notices in the staff common room to show the viewpoint of the schoolmaster; class recordings that tell about teacher–pupil interaction; recorded interviews that demonstrate parents' opinions on the schools and on their children's academic future; and fieldnotes that document Dong Jie's journey in the field; still others that of the teachers, the learners, the parents, the wider community, and so on.

It is one big jigsaw puzzle in which the different bits and types of data have to be put together so as to yield a comprehensive picture. In attempting to solve this puzzle, do keep the image of the cola can in mind: it is the epistemological basis for making your data talk sense.

A subjective image

Pierre Bourdieu's work is complex and voluminous, and it instantiates both the best and the worst of what has come to be known as 'French Theory'. The best is the truly innovative interdisciplinary project he called 'sociology', and which spawned now widely accepted concepts such as *habitus* and *practical sense*. The worst is that much of it only has a textual aesthetic in its language of production, French. Translations of Bourdieu are very often a punishment to the reader. One of the effects of that, unfortunately, is that his work is often read *about* in secondary sources (some but not all of which are very good), and consequently, a lot of what is to be found in his work is left to the avid and studious reader.

This is a pity, for Bourdieu offers us many extremely useful theoretical tools for an ethnographic methodology. It is ethnographic, and Bourdieu himself has underscored that on many occasions (see Blommaert, 2005a; Wacquant, 2004). Bourdieu's work aims at describing social structure – that is, stable macro-features of society – but he does so from within an ethnographic frame in which he looks at situated events and contextualised narratives, analyses these contexts and formulates conclusions about their generalisability. A story he often told was that he was going through photos taken during his fieldwork in Algeria in the early 1960s. He noticed that a photo of a piece of pottery, taken inside a house, was particularly well lit, while he did not have a flash on his camera. The reason why the photo was well lit was that the roof of the house in which it was taken had been blown off by a French grenade. The early 1960s were a period of war in Algeria against French colonial rule, and Bourdieu's early fieldwork was conducted in wartime conditions, in which his own identity as a Frenchman was problematic (see his own reflections in Bourdieu, 2005). It made Bourdieu very much aware of *reflexivity* in research: the way in which the observer has an impact on what is observed, and the way in which the observation events themselves are captured in a real historical context, from which they derive meaning and salience.

Bourdieu's project was *reflexive sociology* and the key to that was *epistemic reflexivity*: the fact that what becomes 'objective' as a scientific *result* is subjective as a scientific *process*. Concretely: in order to be objective one must be subjective (there is no alternative to that), and one must be aware of that subjectivity, that subjectivity must play a role in the way in which one constructs 'objects', that is, objective factual accounts of events.

Your fieldwork materials represent such subjectivity. What they reflect is reality as seen, experienced and understood by you in the learning process described earlier. Your data are as much influenced by real contextual factors as were Bourdieu's photos of pots in demolished houses, and it is your task now to start *using* that subjectivity, that particular situatedness of the knowledge you have gathered, and convert it into an 'objective' account. This raises the issue of generalisability, and we'll have more to say about that in the next section.

To be absolutely clear about this: there is nothing wrong with such subjectivity; it cannot be avoided. As Bourdieu says, it is better to be aware of it and to question what you have seen, heard and understood from within that context, than to pretend that this context wasn't there. There is a lot of social research that does just that: pretend that the research was carried out in a 'context-free' manner; according to Bourdieu, that kind of social research lies.

> It took Dong Jie quite a while to take on board this view, because she came from a strongly positivist background and had believed that research was all about 'objectivity'. She hadn't been fully convinced by the idea of being subjective and context-bounded by the time of entering the field – she even had a fieldwork plan B of quantitative questionnaires and was ready to switch back to her familiar statistics and handy SPSS. However, the schools turned out to be complicated, polycentric, non-black-and-white, and a questionnaire was clearly unable to capture the richness of the space. Moreover, Dong Jie could not claim that she was a researcher who was detached from the researched, because her presence undeniably influenced the pupils (and the teachers) and changed the field that she observed. She also realised that she herself was changed by the people she researched.

She had to come to terms with the reality, and if the process of doing fieldwork was subjective, she must acknowledge it.

So how do you now incorporate this subjectivity into your analysis? First, by examining your data so as to distinguish what is exclusively yours and what could also have been observed and known by others. A simple example: imagine that you witnessed a car crash. This is 'shared' knowledge: many other people will have witnessed it too (although every witness will have experienced it from a different angle). The fact that this crash happened is, therefore, a 'less subjective' given. It could have been known without you being the source of such knowledge, and it would be a 'fact' without you claiming that it is one. Less subjective than, for instance, an entry in your fieldnotes in which you mentioned how uneasy you were in an interview, because the interviewee continuously winked at you and made what you believed were sexually allusive comments. This latter bit of information is 'more subjective' than the previous one: the only way in which it can be known is through your eyes, and it is only a fact because you have interpreted it as such. Distinguishing such degrees of subjectivity is helpful: it assists you in distinguishing between those bits of reality about which you can safely make statements in a factual way, and aspects about which you may wish to be a bit more circumspect, because they may be 'rich points' that tell more about yourself and your own frame of reference than about that of the other. It shapes a clear (or, at least, clearer) zone in which your interpretations need to prevail because they are the only 'data', and they thus create a useful point of departure for systematic checking and counter-checking of your interpretations.

Techniques and Methods

It is impossible to discuss the range of techniques and methods you can use for analysing your data, because essentially, the range is infinite. Every available method can be used to make sense of your data, and your prior training will be your main toolkit. If you have been trained as a linguist, linguistic method – phonetics, morphological analysis – will be your prime instrument for starting to make your data talk. If you were trained as a sociologist, you will probably revert to statistical analysis to quantify some of your data. Other disciplines will bring various other forms of analysis to your data. Jan himself has used a very broad range of analytical approaches to his data, ranging from phonetics to conversation analysis, via historical analysis, syntactic analysis, text analysis, visual analysis – name it. The essence is (but that is easier said than done, of course); use everything that is needed to solve your problems. In the next section, we will give a concrete suggestion on a form of analysis we find particularly interesting and useful: ethnopoetic narrative analysis.

Before embarking on any form of analysis, however, you need to prepare your data for it. It's like in cooking, where the potatoes need to be peeled before they can be cooked. When you have discourse data – interviews, for instance – it is hard to escape the issue of **transcription**. Parts of your data will have to appear in the published report of your research (papers, dissertation), and so what can be heard on tape now needs to be written down. There are good introductory texts on transcription. O'Connell and Kowal (1995) is a very good introduction. Must-reads are also Ochs (1979) and Bucholtz (2000). Both make very important remarks about the way in which transcription is never a perfect 'copy' of the tapes, but always *changes* the discourse, from oral to written, from unremarkable to spectacular sometimes, or vice versa. There is a lot of 'politics' in transcription, argues Bucholtz, because the way in which you transcribe already contains some of your own preferences and biases. This is notably the case with transcribing non-standard speech, where a transcription that uses standard orthography effaces things that could be important elements of social stigma in reality, or, conversely, where transcribing the dialect may stigmatise the speakers. So transcription is never 'neutral' and never 'complete'. There are always things that you will not show in the transcript.

One important thing needs to be kept in mind when you transcribe: it is terribly time-consuming. Even if the result of transcription is that you virtually know the material by heart, it will take a colossal chunk out of your time plan. That is, if you decide to transcribe *everything*. One can be pragmatic about it. Ten hours of recording would easily consume one hundred hours of transcribing; we don't always consider that a wise investment. Instead we make a *précis* of the recordings. We play them and make notes of them, detailed notes in which particular phrases are noted, the topic development is recorded, and certain things are already marked as relevant and worthy of further attention; we also note the particular time point where certain things occur. A typical line would be:

15:45 interesting part 'I don't get nothing, I don't get documents' *

The * marks that this point in the recording (15 minutes and 45 seconds deep in the interview) could be useful for further investigation.

These notes – a 'summary' of the recording – can be consulted whenever we need to find particular data. The collection of such summaries is a precious bit of material. It allows us to quickly survey the recordings, while still having enough detail available to judge accurately what can be useful and what can't. It is on the basis of such summaries that we decide to select particular fragments from the recordings for closer inspection and more refined transcription. This more refined transcription is initially a 'field transcript': a relatively unsophisticated bit of text conventionally organised as 'prose'. Referring back to the line from the summary above, here is the field transcript:

> *So in '95 in September '95 I came here . in . *Belgium .. to Zaventem .... whe I=*when a pass the border I went to the =the city. (?agebedjumuwe?) ask me .. where is my passport .. I say "yeah" . I no get nothing I no get passport . I no get document . they say so if I no get document I for go Salone .. but see de are for no go Salone Salone de were (i) there *boKU::: everybody de die .. so . de all for stay here ... and I went to talk . I ex*plained to *them. what is *happen . and I say yeah . what explain to them is not so *clear . *so I for *go again to =to *talk . (?bu' *may) I sa*bi say .. what *there they *tell *them . is *always that they *tell *them . / but *yeah

In the field transcript, we use a minimum of codes: the asterisk marks stress on the next syllable, the dots mark pauses. We also do not use 'sentences': people don't speak in sentences, as we shall see shortly.

Such transcripts can in turn be infinitely refined, and this is where the disciplinary technique of transcribing enters the picture. Conversation analysis has elaborate techniques for doing so, interactional sociolinguistics likewise, and several other branches of discourse studies also offer specific forms of transcription. Just to give you an idea of what a finished product might look like, here is our final version of what started as the line in our summaries. We show this just to impress you – for explanations on why this fragment has ultimately assumed this shape, please consult Maryns and Blommaert (2001):

1. Setting:

*So in ninety *five   (1)
in Sep*tember ninety *five
I *came here ..
   in . *Belgium ..
   to . *Zaven*tem ....

2. Event narrative:

WHE I= *WHEN a *pass the *border   (2)
I *went to the=the *city .
(?aɣɛbɛjumuwɛ) *ask me .
   where is my passport ..

I say   (3)
    *yeah .
    I *no get nothing
    I *no get passport .
    I *no get document .

they say   (4)
    so if I* no get document
    I for* go Sa*lone ..

3. Commentary:
    But . *see   (5)
    de are for *no go Sa*lone
    =Sa*lone de were (i) there bo*KU::
    *everybody de *die..

    so . de all for *stay here   (6)

4. Refrain:
    and I *went to *talk   (7)
        I ex*plained to *them/. what is *happen .
    and I say ***yeah**
    what I ex*plain to *them is *not *so *clear

    ***so** I for **go a**gain to =to *talk   (8)
    (?b^¿*me:) I sa*bi say
    what *there they *tell *them
    is *always that they *tell *them .

5. Coda:
    but yeah   (9)

So the transcript goes through a number of stages, from very rudimentary to very sophisticated, and every step is a response to a need: you transcribe what you need, and how you need it.

Part of what you will read about the above fragment in Maryns and Blommaert (2001) is that this particular bit of talk had to be transcribed as a narrative. Let us take a closer look at what narratives are.

Analysing Narrative

As said earlier, the 'best' data you could hope for are stories, anecdotes. In such data, we are looking for patterns of narrative and textual coherence. At a trivial level, all texts display some form of coherence, in the sense that they are made out of sequences of meaningful utterances, usually topically organised and shaped by means of a set of formal–textual instruments (grammar, lexis, prosody, intonation, etc.). So in reconstructing the coherence of a text we are trying to decode the meaning of a text.

Two qualifications are in order. First, one has to be on guard for firmly established commonsense connotations of 'coherence' as having to do with strict linearity, logic, structure and clarity in meaning. This interpretation of coherence in itself bears traces of the well-known 'referential ideology' of language (Silverstein, 1979) so widespread in our societies. The 'coherence' referred to here is a minimalistic notion bearing upon the presence of *some* structure and order in texts (and note in passing that 'text' itself is also a very wide notion, obviously not restricted to traditional written textual objects – 'text-artefacts'). There is always *some form of* coherence in texts: some ordering of textual components, some structuring of arguments, some use of communicative resources to mark and distinguish certain parts of a text from others. These forms of textual patterning are forms of coherence, no matter how incoherent they might seem at first.

This is important, because in every culture we do associate forms of coherence with things such as 'truth'. 'Truth' is a metadiscursive concept. Speaking during or in the context of a legal procedure requires swearing 'to tell the truth and nothing but the truth'. Yet, 'truth' is not a property of texts or utterances, but it is an interactionally constructed judgment of value. 'Truth' and 'truthfulness' are textual properties that are attributed and assigned to texts on the basis of the reception of texts. To put it simply, 'truth' does not 'drop off' texts, it is a metadiscursive qualification that needs to be established by interlocutors, and for which interlocutors apply textual and interactional criteria such as absence of contradiction, neat sequentiality of narrative events and episodes, precision, possibility for accurate replication (being able to tell the same story in exactly the same way on different occasions), even-mindedness in the act of telling (*cf.* the famous 'lie-detector', an instrument registering emotions during narration), the possibility to substantiate statements with other textual or non-textual evidence, etc. (see e.g. Briggs, 1997). In our legal procedures, such criteria are crucial in determining the 'truthfulness' and 'reliability' of utterances (statements and testimony). The point, however, is that the criteria used in such acts of evaluation are derived from a strongly literacy-based European understanding of textuality and coherence ('textualism' in Collins' 1996 terms), and that these criteria may clash with the criteria of – text-based – 'truthfulness' and 'reliability' used in societies different from ours.

The point has been stressed on many occasions by Dell Hymes (e.g. 1996). Differences in narrative conventions are rarely 'neutral' and most often accompanied by power differences. Not every language, code, style or narrative mode is equal. Narrative differences go hand in hand with narrative inequalities in which one set of narrative conventions is a source and instrument of power and another is not. A story needs to be told in particular ways, using particular rules of coherence and narrative patterning; if not, it does not qualify as a truthful, reliable, correct story but is discarded as a lie, a figment of the imagination, or an attempt at fraud and manipulation and an expression of the narrator's bad faith. Discovering alternative ways of narrative patterning in stories can be important to uncover hidden modes of oppression and exclusion, based not on truth or falsity *per se* but on truth and falsity as embedded in socioculturally anchored storytelling and interactional practices.

Textual patterns

The central principle in the search for textual patterns of coherence is: language use is a matter of choice. For every expressible thing, people have a variety of ways of expressing it. Differences between such choices are not arbitrary; they involve differences in affect, emotion, emphasis, attitude, feelings and so forth, and they always relate single utterances to wider sociocultural ways of speaking (genres, styles ...). Hence, the precise form taken by an utterance is important; linguistic and pragmatic *shape* is the main entrance to this wider package of social and cultural meanings. This is why we work on live, directly recorded and contextualised (the notebook!) language samples, and this is why transcripts have to be as accurate as possible. Visual inspection of transcripts already reveals textual patterns. Do not *read* transcripts, but *look* at them in the way one looks at a photo or a painting: you will see whether the interlocutors take turns rapidly, where they interrupt and overlap each other in significant ways, whether there are long monologues in the interviews, and most importantly in connection to the foregoing, *where* these features occur in the conversation. The next section will elaborate in greater detail on what happens between speakers in the course of interviews. But here, we can already say that the start and the end of an interview are usually 'marked' parts, that is, parts in which specific patterns occur (brief exchanges, overlaps and interruptions), because in those parts of the interview the participants negotiate roles and expectations. The central parts of an interview also have their own rules, and to these we will now turn.

What counts at the most general level – that the different basic parts of the interview are marked by the participants by means of text-structural features – also counts at a more specific level. Different parts of narratives are marked by different text-structural features, and finding/decoding these differences is a crucial step in understanding how speakers *themselves* 'make sense' (in a most literal sense: making sense requires hard work and permanent effort; 'sense' is manufactured).

We rely heavily on Hymes' ethnopoetics in approaching these issues (see Hymes, 1981, 1996, 1998). Let us quote Hymes at length, stating the 'elementary principles of ethnopoetic analysis' (1996: 166–167, we omit the references made by Hymes and provide occasional clarifications):

1. Performed oral narratives are organised in terms of lines, and groups of lines (not in terms of sentences and paragraphs).

2. The relations between lines and groups of lines are based on the general principle of poetic organisation called equivalence [i.e. the use of 'similarities' and 'differences' in languages] (. . .). Equivalence may involve any feature of language. Features that count to constitute lines are well known: stress, tonal accent, syllable, initial consonant (alliteration), and such forms of equivalence are commonly called metrical [i.e. they have to do with 'poetic meter': the organisation of rhyme schemes, stanza organisation etc.]. Lines of whatever length may also be treated as equivalent in terms of the various forms of rhyme, tone group or intonation contour, initial particles, recurrent syntactic pattern, consistency of contrast of grammatical feature, such as tense or aspect. (. . .)

3. Sequences of equivalent units commonly constitute sets and do so in terms of a few patterned numbers. Sets of two and four are commonly found together in many traditions, as are sets of three and five in others. Where one of these sets is the unmarked pattern, the other pattern may serve to mark emphasis and intensification (. . .). In both the unmarked and marked cases the formative principle is that of arousal and satisfaction of expectation (. . .)

4. Texts are not ordinarily constituted according to a fixed length or fixed sequence of units. Rather, each performance of a narrative may differ from each other, responsive to context and varying intention. The patterning of a text as a whole is an emergent configuration (. . .)

5. Variations and transformations in narratives appear to involve a small number of dimensions, which may prove universal as elements in a model of the mind of the narrator. (. . .)

Important to underscore here is the fact that in this sort of analysis, *any feature of spoken language* can be potentially significant as an element of narrative structuring. Also important is the notion that textual units need not coincide with 'grammatical' units: a narrative unit can consist of parts of a grammatical sentence, or it can cover various sentences. The 'chunking' of a narrative into various units *is performed not by the analyst but from within, by the speakers themselves.* Hence, discovering these units puts us on the track of finding what speakers themselves consider relevant, important and salient in their narrative.[3]

As said above, a text is never 'flat', never completely unified. Speakers always mark certain parts as more relevant than others; they also divide the story into parts, sequentially organised by means of textual markers indicating cohesion between the various parts. Note that in spontaneous, unscripted narrations (i.e. narrations in which the narrator does not rely on notes, documents or a written text), speakers hardly ever start out with a fixed 'plan' of what they will tell. Usually they have an idea of the 'core' of their story. But textual structure is an ongoing thing (in computer terminology: it comes about 'on line'), it is made as the narrator goes along. Remember also that 'coherence' – the ultimate outcome of such structuring work – need not imply perfect logic or linearity.

The identification of textual units is a crucial exercise because it reveals how narrators divide their own story into parts that reflect either phases in a temporally ordered sequence (first this happened, next that ...) and/or greater or lesser relevance, emotion, importance in the story. It is, in other words, one of the few (but most important) leads we have in finding 'emic' ways of narrative structuring.

Let us briefly return to Hymes' quote above, and especially to point (2) of the set of principles of ethnopoetic analysis. In that fragment, Hymes says that 'equivalence' can pertain to 'any feature of language'. In other words, the resources that speakers use to structure their narrative are hard to determine a priori, for they depend on a variety of circumstances. In a moment, we will return to the issue of constraints on resources. But first, the different features that may prove to be relevant in our data can be briefly outlined. We shall distinguish between two types of units: (a) *structural* units, that is, units that have to do with the overall narrative structure of the narrative: sequences, episodes, steps in the reasoning or explanatory process; (b) *relevance* units, that is, units that have to do with marking relevance, importance or sensitivity of what is being told. Both types of units intertwine, and separating them here is done solely for the sake of clarity.

(a) Structural units
   • Explicit temporal anchoring by means of expressions, particles, etc.:
     'then', 'one day', 'in 1994', 'at that time', 'there' (locative and temporal meanings may coincide), ...

- Cohesive particles: 'first', 'next', 'thus', 'so', 'therefore', 'because', 'and', 'also', 'nevertheless', 'and so', ...
- Tense and aspect marking in verbs: past, present, future, conditional, durative, etc. Cohesion is usually marked by means of expressions that carry the same tense/aspect markers.
- Paralinguistic elements: intonation, pitch (loud versus quiet, shouting versus whispering, slow versus fast, calm versus agitated, sighing, pausing ...).
- Finally of course, the sequential and interactional structure: new questions by the interviewer obviously can mark new units in the story. We will return to that later.

(b) Relevance units
  - Lexical choice:
    *'neutral' versus 'marked' terms (lexis): 'rebel' vs. 'Freedom fighter', 'incident' versus 'drama', 'accident' versus 'catastrophe' etc.
    *Euphemisms: 'pass away' versus 'die', 'draw conclusions' versus 'become enemies' etc.
    *the use of comparative and superlative forms: 'bad' versus 'very / extremely bad', 'worse', 'worst'; 'poor' versus 'very / extremely / awfully / outrageously poor'.
    *jargon, group-specific lexis: 'I was taken in custody' versus 'I was arrested, I was caught by the cops, cops put me away' etc.
  - Grammar: agentive versus non-agentive expressions, active versus passive, realis versus irrealis expressions and so forth.
  - Paralinguistic elements: pausing, hesitations, self-corrections, 'loose ends' such as 'etcetera' or 'and so forth'; calls for common ground or solidarity such as 'you see', 'you know', 'you understand'
  - Stylistic units: parallelisms and repetitions marking 'refrains' or 'themes' in the narrative, played dialogue and quoted direct speech or role play, changing (imitating) voices.

Surely, this list is not comprehensive, and more will emerge as we proceed in our analysis. But for the time being, it may be useful to pay particular attention to the occurrence of such elements in the data.

Above, we briefly introduced the issue of constraints on choice. One very important factor, certainly important in our asylum seekers' data, was *competence in the medium of narration*. It does make a difference whether the narrator uses a language or language variety in which s/he is at ease and of which s/he has good control. Narrating in a second, third or other foreign language may considerably reduce the set of resources from which speakers can choose for structuring their story. So, the 'any feature'

referred to by Hymes, will in practice be controlled by all kinds of constraints on availability and accessibility on resources. People who experience difficulties in telling a story in a particular language often make use
of a highly restricted set of linguistic and paralinguistic elements. In such
narratives, we will see the same elements occurring over and over again.

But this does not mean that such stories are 'simple', neither does it
mean that narrators fail to bring about significant degrees of narrative
structure in their stories. Even though the language may be simple and
plain, and despite massive amounts of 'errors' in the language, stories can
be narratively complex and well executed. Let us illustrate this with an
example from asylum seekers' stories. The fragment is taken from the
beginning of an interview with Habiba, a Somali woman who applied for
asylum in Belgium.

H:	I'm from *Somalia and my name is Habiba Mohammed and I=I have *five childrens and I coming here before the children are coming=when I was euh when I=I'm arrive in Belgium I was *alone\
A:	ah\
H:	yeah\in sake of the war=the war of Somalia\
A:	uhuh\
H:	And. I w=I'm. Twen=*thirty five years old\
A:	uhuh\
H:	and euh I was working in Somalia ICRC International red Cross
A:	that's
H:	ICRC *Red Cross\
A:	ah OK OK jaja
B + H:	[acknowledge]
H:	and I was euh office assistant\
A:	ja
H:	yeah. So Somalia is starting war *nineteen ninety one
A:	uhuh\
H:	so until ninety one to ninety five I was in Somalia
A:	uhuh\
H:	and [baby starts crying] wa [laughs] and I have *four children at that time and euhm.. My husband comes from euh *north Somalia
A:	uhuh
H:	and I *south Somalia is fighting north at=at south is fighting\
A:	uhuh
H:	so my=my husband and my children have no. *safety for their lives
A:	uhuh

Habiba clearly has difficulties speaking English. Her statements contain 'calques' (literal translations) such as 'in sake' (line 4, from Dutch 'inzake'), erratic plural marking ('childrens', line 1) and verb inflection ('and I coming here', line 1) and so on. But let us re-transcribe Habiba's narrative, deleting the interviewer's backchannelling interventions as well as the clarification request in lines 9–12. These backchannelling interventions are important, because they support the structuring of Habiba's narrative; but by deleting them we arrive at a number of narrative statements:

1. I'm from *Somalia and my name is Habiba Mohammed and I=I have *five childrens and I coming here before the children are coming=when I was euh when I=I'm arrive in Belgium I was *alone\
2. yeah\in sake of the war=the war of Somalia\
3. and. I w=I'm. Twen=*thirty five years old\
4. and euh I was working in Somalia ICRC International red Cross
5. and I was euh office assistant\
6. So Somalia is starting war *nineteen ninety one
7. so until ninety one to ninety five I was in Somalia
8. and [baby starts crying] wa [laughs] and I have *four children at that time and euhm.. My husband comes from euh *north Somalia
9. and I *south Somalia is fighting north at=at south is fighting\
10. so my=my husband and my children have no. *safety for their lives

There is a considerable degree of narrative structure in this fragment, despite the 'broken' English in which it is made. First, Habiba succeeds in bring in new information in each of her statements. The statements do not overlap; each of them introduces a new element in the story. Also, there is a clear break in this sequence of narrative statements. Although each of the statements adds new information, Habiba marks a thematic break between statements 5 and 6. Statements 1–5 all refer to Habiba herself, they identify her (name, age, country of origin, profession); statements 6–10 are about '[the war in] Somalia' and provide background to the reason why she came to Belgium. The break between both thematic parts is marked by cohesive devices: 'and' in the first part, 'so' (and 'and') in the second. The use of these particles creates a complex pattern of information in the story:

PART I

1. I'm from *Somalia
2. **and** my name is Habiba Mohammed
3. **and** I=I have *five childrens

4. **and** I coming here before the children are coming
　　　{clarification}=when I was euh when I=I'm arrive in Belgium I
　　　was *alone\
　　　yeah\in sake of the war=the war of Somalia\
5. **and**. I w=I'm. Twen=*thirty five years old\
6. **and** euh I was working in Somalia ICRC International red Cross
7. **and** I was euh office assistant\

PART II

1. **So** Somalia is starting war *nineteen ninety one
2. **so** until ninety one to ninety five I was in Somalia
3. **and** [baby starts crying] wa [laughs] and I have *four children at that time
4. **and** euhm.. My husband comes from euh *north Somalia
5. **and** I *south Somalia is fighting north at=at south is fighting\
6. **so** my=my husband and my children have no. *safety for their lives

We can go a bit further. In part II, two levels can be distinguished. Not all the statements in part II are equally relevant. Statements 1, 2 and 6 are 'main statements', setting important argumentative and narrative frames. Statement 1 introduces the general historical frame of the war in Somalia; statement 2 places Habiba in that historical frame, and statement 6 draws a general conclusion from this general sketch of Habiba's family's situation in the war. Statements 3, 4 and 5 elaborate on statement 2: they clarify and specify statement 2, Habiba (and her family) living in Somalia during the war years. Thus, we arrive at the following structure for part II:

PART II

1. **So** Somalia is starting war *nineteen ninety one
2. **so** until ninety one to ninety five I was in Somalia
　　3. **and** [baby starts crying] wa [laughs] and I have *four children at that time
　　4. **and** euhm.. My husband comes from euh *north Somalia
　　5. **and** I *south Somalia is fighting north at=at south is fighting\
6. **so** my=my husband and my children have no. *safety for their lives

The main statements are marked by 'so'; the subordinate ones by 'and'. The structure is crystal clear, and Habiba accomplishes it by means of only two cohesive markers: 'and' and 'so'. Conclusion: stories told in 'simple' language are not necessarily 'simple' stories.

Let us now return to the general issue of marking narrative units. Cohesive devices such as particles are clear elements of unit marking, as we have seen in Habiba's example. But at a more general level, units may be marked by complex sets of features – put simply, different units may be marked by completely different ways of speaking. Parts of the story can be told in slow, long, circumspect utterances; other parts can be told in fast, emotional or agitated speech; parts of the story can be told in long spontaneously offered narratives; other parts can be told in brief matter-of-fact like answers to questions, without any elaboration or extra, unsolicited, information.

The interviewer's impact on this can be great, as we have seen earlier. The interviewer can raise issues in questions that are *Gefundenes Fressen* for the interviewee, about which s/he is willing to talk at length, enthusiastically and in great detail. But the interviewer can also raise issues that are experienced as delicate, sensitive, difficult to tell and so on by the interviewee. The interviewee displays these attitudes towards this issue by a completely different talking style: brief, yes/no answers, evasive statements, euphemisms, long pauses, shifting the initiative to the interviewer ('Is there anything else you want to know?', 'Any more questions?'), hesitations and self-corrections.

The following fragments are taken from an interview with Didier, a Congolese refugee in Belgium. The whole first half of the interview was characterised by a rather dismissive and uncooperative attitude of Didier vis-à-vis the interviewers (two young Belgian women, V and T). After having given another answer, Didier stops abruptly and the interviewers are forced to take the initiative. Note that the interview is done in French, a language in which D appears considerably more comfortable than V and T:

[pause]
V: {to T, in Dutch} okay\ what else did you want to ask [pause]
T: (x) I can really (x)
V: ehrm
V do you have ehrm a house here\ a life
D: [question intonation] yes
T: do you have a house here\ a life
D: yes I have a house
T: hm
V: a house and\ a job\ aaand
D: a house=I *rent a house\\ yes
T: yes
V: So you work
D: no I don't work\\ I already mentioned that I used to work\ but I had
        a problem with the *permit

T: yes\ and what=what do you live on (then)
D   (me personally) \ I live off the OCMW \ but (not long)\ (xx) because
       me\ I am still in the procedure
V   {introduces new topic}

The initiative to keep the interview going is continuously shifted to
the interviewers by Didier. He answers the questions directly and in an
informative way, but after each question he leaves the floor to the interviewers. It is clear that Didier doesn't fancy talking a lot about the topics
raised by the interviewers. But later on in the same interview, Didier
shifts into a completely different mode of speech. At one point, Didier
says 'I'm here to help the people' (the interview was recorded in a church
occupied by asylum seekers). From that point onwards, he takes full
initiative, and the interviewers have a hard time getting a word in
edgewise:

D: But he=here\I am here to help the people a bit
T: mhm
D: I know that\for at least (more than) five years I know many people
       here\ who are without...*means one must help them *always\\ but
       here we are already in a community\\ I am (here already) in a
       community\\ here this community there are people who have no
       papers they have to be supported\\ it's like everywhere abroad\
       there are Belgian communities
A: but=
D: =it exists\ there will be an Antwerp community if you go there ehr\
       (x)\ it exists
A: but it is also a community (the people xx)=
D: [but of course\ there's a community\
                                            there are many Zairians who are here
A: yes I know but=
D: yeah\ there is this community\ even if it has no eherm *structure\
       there's a president and everything\ it's=that community exists

The brief and measured sentences of the first fragment have disap-
peared and have been replaced by an agitated style of speaking. The interviewer tries to intervene in lines 7, 9 and 12; twice her attempts fail (lines
7 and 12), once she succeeds but is cut short by Didier (9). Clearly, such
overall stylistic differences indicate more than just funny ways of talking
to interviewers: they indicate topics, themes, parts of the story that are
different from foregoing and following parts.

Identifying argumentative/explanatory patterns

Closely connected to the previous comments is the division of texts into argumentative or explanatory patterns. Emphasis, logical or associative sequences; cause–effect relations, argument–elaboration patterns are all marked by speakers. In order to make their point, speakers draw upon complex sets of related arguments, illustrations, conclusions, deductions and so forth. Let us take a look at an example. The following fragment is taken from an interview with an Angolese couple of refugees (husband = P; wife = D); the interviewer is GM. The interview was in French.

GM   And for instance TV programs/ do you think they help your case?
D   [well it's hard to say==one can=
GM   [the programs we have seen
P   ==no no no
GM   'cause as soon as it's been on TV/ the whole of Belgium has seen it=
P   =yeah
GM   [so
D   [==but
GM   surely they couldn't send you back
P   buuut/ it's=it's what they say it=it's=OOKAAY
D   we've seen but afterwards they've changed here==
P   ==normally==
D   ==on the TV they say/ ooh noo/ we can't give to all the people after five years the=we've done ehr ten years/ things like that/ we'll have a look at the procedures/ but the first day they said on TV/ ooh noo/ we'll give to the people who they've done five years in our country because there were children who we=went to school here for some time/ we've done six years=five years and the children they go to school==it's the Mayor of Brussels who said that=
GM   =hmm=
D   =yeah/ they children they have integrated here since long=they go to school but now I think that they'll give them the=to give to the children=there to their parents/ *but after a few days they said/ oohh nooo we will ehr=follow the procedures [hits hands on thighs] BUT *HOW CAN WE FOLLOW THE PROCEDURES? [annoyed] *since I arrived here in Belgium I've got no papers/ do you follow me?/ no papers/ here/ example/ not for me for the moment/ there comes here like a=there's a woman here in the newspaper=yesterday=we have read/ people without documents/came here/ he's got three children==five children here in Belgium/ seven years=six years without

documents/ so/ at that moment you say/ got to follow the procedures/ that woman there/ since the summer you have e=u the proce=the documents/ you have thrown away that woman's documents/ we don't know what's=wh=procedure/ *what procedure one can follow/ for the woman? That is the problems/ the *Belgians cannot give to the people th=documents just like that/ they think that they give/ *aaahh all these people stay in our country/ but eh=*so long they leaves to countries of the people to stay there/ in *Portugal there are Belgians=they have done something there/ at=in Zaire there are many=

P   =in Angola

The Angolese woman, D, tries to make a point here, and a crucial point in understanding her condition and experiences as a refugee: the gap between what Belgians believe happens to refugees, and what really happens to them in Belgium. She makes this point in very broken French, part of the features of which do not appear in the English version (e.g. ambiguous 3rd person '*on*', meaning 'they' as well as 'us' and impersonal 'one'). But just as what we saw before in the case of Habiba, the difficulties D has with expressing herself in grammatically correct French tend to obscure the elaborate argumentative structure of D's talk.

Prompted by GM's suggestion (lines 1, 5, 9) that TV exposure would create a more favourable climate for asylum seekers to obtain their documents (i.e. to be 'regularised' and given legal residence permits) she argues that this is not the case. She describes what happened. First, largely in quoted direct speech ('ooh noo') she describes how the Mayor of Brussels declared on TV that people with children who go to school in Belgium and who have been in the country for years would be regularised. This is done in lines 13–18, and recapitulated in lines 20–21. Next she describes how the Belgian authorities shift their position a couple of days later, again using quoted direct speech (line 21). She then presents her own opinion: 'but how can we follow the procedures?', and then starts elaborating on that theme, using an anecdote picked up from the newspaper, of a woman who had been here for years and lived here with her children. This then leads to a conclusion and a coda, in which the situation of asylum seekers in Belgium is compared to the freedom with which Belgians settle elsewhere in the world.

Despite her 'broken' French, D constructs a clear pattern of arguments, schematically represented as follows. Note also how the central motif of the argument, the issue of how to follow procedures, is marked by parallelisms (indicated by arrows ⇐):

1. Background:
They will give the [documents] to the children to their parents
    because they have been integrated here (says the Mayor of Brussels)

2. Point of departure:
[BUT] afterwards they say that we have to follow the procedures ⇐

3. Refutation
    3.1. Core
    But how can we follow the procedures? ⇐
    3.2. Elaboration
    1. Ever since I arrived here, I lived without documents
    2. Anecdote: *Report*
                  yesterday we have read in the newspaper
                  A woman with no documents and 3/5 children
                  No documents for 7/6 years

                  Comment
                  And then they say that you have to follow the procedure ⇐
                  [BUT] you have thrown away that woman's documents
                      We don't know what procedure to follow ⇐

4. Conclusion and coda
That is the problem
    The Belgians cannot give documents just like that [i.e. they *don't* give papers just like that, procedures must be followed, and this is problematic]
    [BUT] Belgians believe that everyone just stays in their country
    [WHILE] Belgians themselves can be found all over the world (Portugal, Zaire, Angola)

Just like in Habiba's case, we see a well-organised narrative pattern emerge over and beyond difficulties in handling the medium of narration. The core of the argument is clearly marked, and the refutation is accomplished by means of comparison of D's situation with that of someone else (the anecdote) and leads to a convincing point: staying in Belgium is not as simple as Belgians tend to believe it is; in fact, Belgians have an easier time when they decide to go and live abroad.

The result

We have seen similar things in earlier examples as well. Anecdotes, small stories, contain complex patterns that lead us right into the experiential world of the storyteller: his/her cultural and social codes, feeling about what is told, own position vis-à-vis the topic of the story, and so forth. It is an immensely rich complex of meanings, for which a fine-grained and sensitive analysis is required. Such an analysis needs to look beyond the surface of stories and has to delve into the fabric of stories: their implicit structure, the often invisible codes and rules that structure them. If we follow Hymes, such codes and rules are deeply cultural, *because* they are implicit. Looking for such structures, therefore, brings out the best from your data.

Remember the motto we used at the beginning of this book, where Hymes warned us about

the small portion of cultural behavior that people can be expected to report or describe, when asked, and the much smaller portion that an average person can be expected to manifest by doing on demand.

The narrative analysis sketched here is a technique that recognises this problem: the meanings that people produce are not all explicit, cannot all be 'read off' their words; they need to be extracted, excavated. Doing so yields a rich harvest of insights.

Notes

1. In Dutch, we often use a jargon word for this: 'ontluizen', that is, getting rid of lice and other bugs. People may find you a strange character immediately after a protracted and intense fieldwork period. You must realise that you have indeed been immersed in a very strange set of social activities. Reconnecting with friends, partners and family is not always easy.
2. There is a tradition of using 'data' as a singular noun, as in 'The data for this paper is a piece of recording . . .'. We prefer to use it etymologically as a *plural* noun, the plural of Latin 'datum'.
3. The attentive reader has already concluded at this point that we are continuously shifting here between linguistic and metalinguistic levels. Elements of linguistic structuring are being used for metalinguistic functions: to add meanings, attitudes, feelings, affect, etc. that cannot be expressed by words alone.

Read up on it

Bamberg, M. (ed.) (2006) *Narrative – State of the Art*. Amsterdam: John Benjamins (special issue of *Narrative Inquiry* 16/1).

Blommaert, J. (2004) *Workshopping: Professional Vision, Practices and Critique in Discourse Analysis*. Ghent: Academia.

Blommaert, J. (2006) Ethnopoetics as functional reconstruction: Dell Hymes' narrative view of the world. *Functions of Language* 13 (2), 229–249.

Fabian, J. (2001) *Anthropology with an Attitude*. Stanford: Stanford University Press.

Hymes, D. (1981) *In Vain I Tried to Tell you: Essays in Native American Ethnopoetics*. Philadelphia: University of Pennsylvania Press.

Ochs, E. and Capps, L. (2001) *Living Narrative. Creating Lives in Everyday Storytelling*. Cambridge, MA: Harvard University Press.

Wacquant, L. (ed.) (2004) *Pierre Bourdieu in the Field*. London: Sage (special issue of *Ethnography* 5/4).

Werner, O. and Schoepfle, M. (1987b) *Systematic Fieldwork Volume 2: Ethnographic Analysis and Data Management*. Newbury Park: Sage.

Chapter 6
Postscript

Where are we now – what do we know that we didn't know before? We hope that we know at least

(1) That ethnographic fieldwork is grounded in an epistemological and methodological framework that sets it apart from most other approaches in the social sciences. It is not just a *technique*, but it is part of a *theoretical complex*, a paradigm, of considerable sophistication. It is the theoretical background that makes fieldwork a scientifically valid enterprise – if it is done well.

(2) We also hope that we know that doing fieldwork well revolves around understanding what it is you are doing. You are, in fieldwork, constructing an archive of your own learning process; that means: you are gathering a 'subjective', interpretive collection of evidence that reflexively tells a story about social roles, social positions, social events: the walk around the can of coke on the table. Everything in this collection of evidence is situated, contextualised, and your work is aimed at understanding the contextualised nature of events. You will try to understand the totality of contexts, not just a selection of them – remember the metaphor of the football game. You are trying to describe and understand complexity – not simplification.

(3) In so doing, you deploy a wide variety of research activities, resulting in 'data' of very different kinds – from very 'objective' things (e.g. publicly available documents) to very 'subjective' ones (e.g. your field-notes). These data together offer you pieces of a jigsaw puzzle. Solving the puzzle is the work of analysis, and it is an attempt at constructing a *replica* of what you witnessed and experienced. Ethnography is the science that explicitly attempts to be *iconic* in relation to its object: an ethnographic analysis will attempt to 'mirror' the events and processes it describes. If these are complex, the analysis is complex; if they contained paradoxes, such paradoxes will also emerge in the analysis.

That much is clear. It is also clear that reading this book does not mean that you are ready for the real thing now. You never will be ready; even experienced fieldworkers feel overwhelmed and at a loss when they begin a new piece of fieldwork. As said above, chaos is the state of things. You are not ready, but you may be slightly better prepared for the chaos and the perceived lack of structure and transparency that you will encounter (and that so clashes with the elegance of your research proposal!). The points raised and offered in this book are points for reflection, not immediate, practical solutions. They can be seen as *complicating* suggestions, things that make it even harder. But – in the end, they should be practical and useful. For if fieldwork doesn't start from assumptions of complexity, it is bound to miss the whole point.

References

Blommaert, J. (2001) Context is/as critique. *Critique of Anthropology* 21 (1), 13–32.

Blommaert, J. (2004) *Workshopping: Professional Vision, Practices and Critique in Discourse Analysis*. Ghent: Academia.

Blommaert, J. (2005a) Bourdieu the ethnographer: The ethnographic grounding of habitus and voice. *The Translator* 11 (2), 219–236.

Blommaert, J. (2005b) *Discourse: A Critical Introduction*. Cambridge: Cambridge University Press.

Blommaert, J. (ed.) (1999) *Language Ideological Debates*. Berlin: Mouton de Gruyter.

Blommaert, J. and Bulcaen, C. (2000) Critical discourse analysis. *Annual Review of Anthropology* 29, 447–466.

Blommaert, J. and Verschueren, J. (1998) *Debating Diversity: Analysing the Discourse of Tolerance*. London: Routledge.

Blommaert, J., Collins, J., Heller, M., Rampton, B., Slembrouck, S. and Verschueren, J. (eds) (2001) *Discourse and Critique*. Special double issue, *Critique of Anthropology* 21 (1&2).

Bourdieu, P. (1990) *The Logic of Practice*. Cambridge: Polity Press.

Bourdieu, P. (2005) Algerian landing. *Ethnography* 5 (4), 415–443.

Briggs, C. (1986) *Learning How to Ask*. Cambridge: Cambridge University Press.

Briggs, C. (1997) Notes on a 'confession': On the construction of gender, sexuality and violence in an infanticide case. *Pragmatics* 7, 519–546.

Bucholtz, M. (2000) The politics of transcription. *Journal of Pragmatics* 32, 1439–1465.

Clifford, J. (1988) *The Predicament of Culture: Twentieth-Century Ethnography, Literature and Art*. Cambridge: Harvard University Press.

Cook-Gumperz, J. (ed.) (1988) *The Social Construction of Literacy*. Cambridge: Cambridge University Press.

Darnell, R. (1998) *And Along Came Boas. Continuity and Revolution in Americanist Anthropology*. Amsterdam: John Benjamins.

Fabian, J. (1979) (1991) Rule and process. In J. Fabian (ed.) *Time and the Work of Anthropology* (pp. 87–109). Chur: Harwood.

Fabian, J. (1983) *Time and the Other. How Anthropology Makes Its Object*. New York: Columbia University Press.

Fabian, J. (1986) *Language and Colonial Power*. Cambridge: Cambridge University Press.

Fabian, J. (1995) Ethnographic misunderstanding and the perils of context. *American Anthropologist* 97 (1), 41–50.

Fabian, J. (1996) *Remembering the Present*. Berkeley: University of California Press.

Gee, J. (1996) *Social Linguistics and Literacies*. London: Taylor & Francis.

Ginzburg, C. (1989) *Clues, Myths, and the Historical Method*. Baltimore: Johns Hopkins University Press.

Goffman, E. (1971) *Relations in Public: Microstudies of the Public Order*. New York: Harper & Row.

Gumperz, J. (1968) The speech community. *International Encyclopaedia of the Social Sciences* (pp. 381–386). New York: Macmillan. Reprinted in A. Duranti (ed.) 2001. *Linguistic Anthropology: A Reader* (pp. 43–52). London: Blackwell.

Heller, M. (2000) *Linguistic Minorities in Late Modernity*. London: Longman.

Hymes, D. (1964) *Language in Culture and Society. A Reader in Linguistics and Anthropology*. New York: Harper & Row.

Hymes, D. 1972 (1986) Models of the interaction of language and social life. In J. Gumperz and D. Hymes (eds) *Directions in Sociolinguistics: The Ethnography of Communication* (pp. 35–71). London: Basil Blackwell.

Hymes, D. (1980) What is ethnography. In D. Hymes (ed.) *Language in Education: Ethnolinguistic Essays* (pp. 88–103). Washington, DC: Center for Applied Linguistics.

Hymes, D. (ed.) (1981) *In Vain I Tried to Tell You: Essays in Native American Ethnopoetics*. Philadelphia: University of Pennsylvania Press.

Hymes, D. (1983) *Essays in the History of Linguistic Anthropology*. Amsterdam: John Benjamins.

Hymes, D. (1996) *Ethnography, Linguistics, Narrative Inequality: Toward an Understanding of Voice*. London: Taylor & Francis.

Kroskrity, P. (ed.) (2000) *Regimes of Language*. Santa Fe: SAR Press.

Maryns, K. (2006) *The Asylum Speaker: Language in the Belgian Asylum Procedure*. Manchester: Encounters.

Maryns, K. and Blommaert, J. (2001) Stylistic and thematic shifting as a narrative resource: Assessing asylum seekers' repertoires. *Multilingua* 20, 61–84.

Ochs, E. (1979) Transcription as theory. In E. Ochs and B. Schieffelin (eds) *Developmental Pragmatics* (pp. 43–72). New York: Academic Press.

O'Connell, D. and Kowal, S. (1995) Transcription systems for spoken discourse. In J. Verschueren, J-O. Ostman and J. Blommaert (eds) *Handbook of Pragmatics: Manual* (pp. 646–656). Amsterdam: John Benjamins.

Rampton, B. (1995) *Crossing: Language and Ethnicity among Adolescents*. London: Longman.

Sapir, E. (1929) The status of linguistics as a science. *Language* 5, 207–214.

Silverstein, M. (1979) Language structure and linguistic ideology. In P. Clyne, W. Hanks and C. Hofbauer (eds) *The Elements: A Parasession on Linguistic Units and Levels* (pp. 193–247). Chicago: Chicago Linguistic Society.

Silverstein, M. and Urban, G. (eds) (1996) *Natural Histories of Discourse*. Chicago: University of Chicago Press.

Stocking, G. (1992) *The Ethnographer's Magic and Other Essays in the History of Anthropology*. Madison: University of Wisconsin Press.

Verschueren, J. (1995) The pragmatic perspective. In J. Verschueren, J-O. Östman and J. Blommaert (eds) *Handbook of Pragmatics: Manual* (pp. 1–19). Amsterdam: John Benjamins.

Wacquant, L. (2005) Following Pierre Bourdieu in the field. *Ethnography* 5, 387–414.

Woolard, K., Schieffelin, B. and Kroskrity, P. (eds) (1998) *Language Ideologies: Theory and Practice*. New York: Oxford University Press.

Index